REVELS STUDENT EDITIONS

THE TAMER TAMED;
OR, THE WOMAN'S PRIZE
John Fletcher

MANCHESTER
1824

Manchester University Press

REVELS STUDENT EDITIONS

Based on the highly respected Revels Plays, which provide a wide range of scholarly critical editions of plays by Shakespeare's contemporaries, the Revels Student Editions offer readable and competitively priced introductions, text and commentary designed to distil the erudition and insights of the Revels Plays, while focusing on matters of clarity and interpretation. These editions are aimed at undergraduates, graduate teachers of Renaissance drama and all those who enjoy the vitality and humour of one of the world's greatest periods of drama.

GENERAL EDITOR David Bevington

Dekker/Rowley/Ford *The Witch of Edmonton*
Ford *'Tis Pity She's a Whore*
Jonson *Volpone Bartholomew Fair*
Kyd *The Spanish Tragedy*
Marlowe *The Jew of Malta Tamburlaine the Great*
Marston *The Malcontent*
Middleton/Rowley *The Changeling*
Middleton/Tourneur *The Revenger's Tragedy*
Webster *The Duchess of Malfi The White Devil*

Plays on Women: An Anthology
Middleton *A Chaste Maid in Cheapside*
Middleton/Dekker *The Roaring Girl*
Anon. *Arden of Faversham*
Heywood *A Woman Killed with Kindness*

REVELS STUDENT EDITIONS

THE TAMER TAMED;
OR, THE WOMAN'S
PRIZE

John Fletcher

edited by Celia R. Daileader and Gary Taylor

MANCHESTER
UNIVERSITY PRESS

Introduction, critical apparatus, etc.
© Celia R. Daileader and Gary Taylor 2006

The right of Celia R. Daileader and Gary Taylor to be identified as the
editors of this work has been asserted by them in accordance with the
Copyright, Designs and Patents Act 1988.

Published by Manchester University Press
Altrincham Street, Manchester M1 7JA, UK
www.manchesteruniversitypress.co.uk

British Library Cataloguing-in-Publication Data
A catalogue record for this book is available from the British Library

ISBN 978 0 7190 5367 2 paperback

First published 2006

Typeset by SNP Best-set Typesetter Ltd, Hong Kong

Introduction

There have been poets who let something different from tradition get through at any price . . . men able to think the woman who would resist destruction and constitute herself as a superb, equal, 'impossible' subject. (Hélène Cixous)[1]

Sometimes only a man can afford to be a feminist.

John Fletcher (1579–1625), writing in an age when notions of male supremacy were virtually unchallenged, was just such a man. His play *The Tamer Tamed* answers and inverts Shakespeare's misogynist masterwork, *The Taming of the Shrew*. The 'comic resolution' of Shakespeare's play is a husband's unqualified squelching of his wife's formerly outspoken and spirited nature. However at odds with modern notions of egalitarian marriage and gender equity, *The Taming of the Shrew* belongs to a long tradition of wife 'taming' literature, from Punch and Judy to anonymous ballads, which endorses a husband's right to exercise violence in bringing a rebellious wife under control.

What enabled John Fletcher to see the inhumanity in these traditional paradigms? His biography furnishes some clues. Although his older brother followed father and grandfather Fletcher into the Anglican ministry, John did not. Perhaps by 1606, certainly by 1607, he was associating with the London literary circle of Ben Jonson and Sir Francis Beaumont. By 1613 Beaumont and Fletcher had co-written six to ten plays, including the enormously popular comedy *The Scornful Lady*, which was published in eight editions by 1660 (more than any Shakespeare play except *Henry the Fourth, Part One*).[2] They quickly became the most famous partnership in the English theatre, and they retained that status until late in the nineteenth century, when they were finally eclipsed by Gilbert and Sullivan. According to later gossip, Fletcher and Beaumont 'lived together on the Bankside, not far from the playhouse, both bachelors; lay together . . . had one wench in the house between them, which they did so admire; the same clothes and cloak, etc., between them'.[3] Whatever the truth, the relationship between the two men was so close that it was suspected of being sexual. Their alleged

1

ménage-à-trois with a shared 'wench' also scandalously violated the sanctities of monogamy. Fletcher was, in more than one respect, a 'sexual dissident'.[4]

Beaumont married a rich heiress and suffered a stroke in 1613, stopped writing plays, and died in 1616; he was buried in Westminster Abbey, joining the canonical company of Chaucer and Spenser. Fletcher never married, and never stopped writing. Even during his Beaumont years, he wrote plays entirely on his own, including *The Tamer Tamed*. Nevertheless, even in a collaborative age and a collaborative theatrical milieu, Fletcher was exceptionally fond of creative partnerships. His favorite collaborator, after Beaumont, was Philip Massinger (1583–1640), who had himself buried in the same grave as Fletcher, fifteen years after Fletcher's death.[5] But Fletcher did not confine himself to Massinger. Between 1612 and 1625 he teamed up with many other writers, including the actor-playwrights William Shakespeare, Nathan Field, and William Rowley. Lacking any personal experience of marriage, Fletcher imagined it, at its best, as a relationship like those between male collaborators: a 'due equality' that requires and enables both parties 'to love mutually' (5.4.97–8).

This is not to say that Fletcher's female characters had no female counterparts in Fletcher's life. His most important patrons were Henry Hastings (the fifth Earl of Huntington) and his wife Elizabeth Stanley. Fletcher shared with the Earl and Countess of Huntington a distaste for political absolutism – including, apparently, the absolutism of traditional patriarchal marriage, which lets men 'reign as tyrants o'er their wives' (Epi.4). Gordon McMullan has described the Huntington household as 'feminocentric', and the Earl himself praised his wife for her 'judicious conceit and masculine understanding'.[6] Others called her 'learneder than Hypatia' (the ancient female mathematician), and observed that few women paid 'so close an attention as she had generally done to reading'.[7] Fletcher's only surviving letter to his patrons is a verse epistle to Elizabeth, comparing her to 'Eve before the fall' and claiming her as the 'original' of his 'all'.[8]

Elizabeth Stanley may have inspired plays, but she did not write them. Women were systematically excluded from the institutions in which men competed with each other: not only theatres but grammar schools, universities, athletic contests, chivalric rituals, wars. Today a woman can win the Nobel and the Pulitzer Prize, win an election, win an Olympic gold medal. But in Elizabeth

Stanley's world there were literally no prizes that a woman could win, because there were none for which she was allowed to compete. That is why *The Tamer Tamed* has an alternative, equally paradoxical title: *The Woman's Prize* is an oxymoron, because every prize in early modern Europe was a man's prize. The prowess of the play's female protagonist has to be troped in the male terms of warfare, jousting, and the competitive rhetorical exercises of a humanist education.

Like the real Elizabeth Stanley, the fictional Maria, Fletcher's heroine, could win only metaphorical wars and metaphorical prizes. In any case, for decades the role of Maria was not even performed by a woman. Until 1660 the English stage was a male domain, with all women's parts written and played by males. Women who might have challenged that monopoly, from Elizabeth Cary to Margaret Cavendish, employed their female pens in writing disembodied closet drama. Cary's sole surviving dramatic text, *The Tragedy of Mariam, Fair Queen of Jewry* (1613), has recently been canonized by feminist scholars. But although every feminist must applaud the effort to recover lost female voices, we cannot expect all those voices to sound the same, or to share our own opinions – or to express our opinions even if they secretly shared them.[9] *Mariam* itself is not a very encouraging feminist fable. It concerns itself with competition between women for the favour of a tyrannical male; in typical patriarchal fashion, it damns most women in order to celebrate one singularly chaste paragon; it contrasts its 'fair' (pale-skinned) heroine with vicious women whose bodies are 'brown' and 'black'.[10] Fletcher's stage-play, by contrast, celebrates collective female insurrection against male power, and its few ethnocentric slurs are all spoken by sexually threatened males. And whereas Cary's heroine dies at the hands of her royal lover, Fletcher's heroine triumphs in the end, having 'tamed' her hitherto domineering husband. Fletcher, as a man, could boldly go where no woman in 1610 dared to tread: on to a feminist stage.

CENSORSHIP

In fact, though, even men might find themselves in trouble for going where Fletcher went. Although *The Tamer Tamed* was probably written between November 1609 and February 1610, the first indisputable reference to it is a government document written on the morning of 18 October 1633, when Sir Henry Herbert 'sent a warrant by a messenger of the chamber to suppress *The Tamer Tamed*, to the King's players, for that afternoon'. Herbert was Master of the Revels, the court official responsible for licensing and censoring every theatrical performance; a Messenger of the (Privy) Chamber was a legal representative of the most powerful committee of the government, which combined both executive and judicial powers; 'the King's players' (also known as the King's Men) were the most successful and secure acting company in England. Herbert's warrant forbade 'the acting of your play called *The Tamer Tamed*, or *The Taming of the Tamer*, this afternoon, or any more till you have leave from me – and this at your peril'. This ban, terminating in an explicit threat, had been prompted by 'complaints of foul and offensive matters contained therein'. The next day the actors sent Herbert 'the book' (the previously licensed manuscript of the play), and two days later he returned it to the players 'purged of oaths, profaneness, and ribaldry'.

Whatever the particulars that offended Herbert, the specific complaint about *The Tamer Tamed* generated a more global anxiety about revivals of old plays. Herbert had been licensing plays for over eleven years, but he now felt it necessary to change the rules of the game:

> All old plays ought to be brought to the Master of the Revels . . . since they may be full of offensive things against church and state; the rather that in former times the poets took greater liberty than is allowed them by me.

He then concludes that 'The players ought not to study their parts' until he had licensed the play.[11]

The Tamer Tamed created, in 1633, a seismic disturbance in the relationship between the acting companies and the censor. In part, Herbert's extreme reaction to the play may have been due (as Richard Dutton suggests) to bad timing: between November 1632 and 24 October 1633 Herbert found himself repeatedly accused by his superiors (including particularly the Archbishop of Canterbury, William Laud) of being excessively lenient or careless in licensing objectionable texts.[12] But Herbert did not initiate this affair; instead, he was reacting to a 'complaint' against the play made by someone else. His reading of the manuscript then generated a more general prohibition on reviving old plays without relicensing them.

Fortunately, we can trace and to some extent undo what censorship did to *The Tamer Tamed* because we possess two distinct early texts. The play was included – with the title *The Woman's Prize: or,*

The Tamer Tamed – in the 1647 folio edition of thirty-four *Comedies and Tragedies* attributed to Beaumont and Fletcher. That text apparently derives from the licensed playbook that Herbert returned to the King's Men, 'purged of oaths, profaneness, and ribaldry'. But an undated, untitled seventeenth-century manuscript of the play also survives (now in the Folger library). This manuscript seems to have been copied for a patron or paying customer, someone who had seen or heard about the play and wanted to read it, before it was printed. Like the printed text of 1647, the manuscript also apparently derives from the licensed playbook owned by the King's Men – but it seems to have been copied from that source *before* the playbook was handed over to Herbert on 19 October 1633. Consequently, the manuscript makes it possible to restore many of the 'offensive things' Herbert removed. Our edition is based primarily on the manuscript; we also conjecturally supply a few Fletcherian oaths (placed in square brackets) that seem to have been removed from both early texts. Our edition is, as a result, more 'offensive' than any previous printed text of the play.

The offensiveness of Fletcher's play can be divided into three categories: vulgarity, blasphemy, and subversion. All three are central to the play's literary achievement and to its representation of the 'bond' of matrimony.

The play Fletcher wanted audiences to hear is artfully vulgar, bawdy, smutty, scatological, even gross. It does not romanticize, euphemize, or sanitize the bodily functions central to gender ideology and conflict. It flouts the standards of good taste.[13] Nevertheless, scholars who focus only on the censorship of the play's vulgarity are bound to be puzzled by inconsistencies. For instance, Herbert cut 'piss' (1.1.46) and 'piss-pots' (App. 4.0.2), but passed over 'pissed' (5.1.66); he cut a reference to Petruccio's 'tools' (3.3.155), but left intact the joke about the young lover Roland kissing his sweetheart Livia's '(w)hole' (5.1.22). N. W. Bawcutt seems to feel that Herbert had undertaken a Herculean labour in censoring such 'ribaldry', as Fletcher's text 'contains so many double meanings that to remove them would destroy the play'.[14] But double entendre was not, in itself, objectionable. As long as the gross meaning 'hole' was decently covered by the polite spelling 'whole', Herbert could live with it. But there was no such camouflage for *piss* (on the first page of the play) and *tools* (which in context can have no asexual meaning). Herbert's words and his actions make it clear that, by 1633, public 'ribaldry' and 'obsceneness' were being policed by at least one comptroller of poetic licence. Herbert's attitude anticipated the modern Anglo-American obsession with regulating sexual expression.

However, in general what we might call obscenity was less likely to be censored than blasphemous religious speech.[15] In May 1606 Parliament had passed legislation 'For the preventing and avoiding of the great Abuse of the Holy Name of God in stage plays', which imposed a penalty of £10 on 'any person or persons' in a theatrical performance who dared 'jestingly or profanely speak or use the holy Name of God'.[16] Some playwrights scrupulously obeyed this law; others ignored it. The word 'God' appears almost four hundred times in the original editions of Fletcher's plays. Whatever the actors dared to speak on stage, Fletcher regarded 'God' as an essential component of idiomatic English speech. Indeed, 'God' is the first word spoken in *The Tamer Tamed*: 'God give 'em joy!'

This first speech illustrates an important fact about early modern censorship. 'God' is the reading of the 1647 printed edition, deriving from the text that Herbert had 'purged' in 1633. By contrast, the earlier manuscript text has a common euphemism ('Heaven'), often inserted to replace the forbidden word 'God'. The manuscript euphemism is not really surprising, because the play had already been submitted to the original censor (Sir George Buc) before its first performances. But if 'God' was expurgated in 1609–10, why does it survive in a text printed in 1647, from a manuscript more thoroughly expurgated in 1633? The answer is suggested by the publisher's preface to the 1647 folio, which brags that 'now you have both All that was *Acted*, and all that was not; even the perfect full Originals without the least mutilation'. Thus, the 1647 edition may have deliberately restored some of the profanity of Fletcher's original. Anyone working from the original playbook may have been able to read the original 'God', crossed out and replaced by 'Heaven'. When the 1647 editor could read the original, he preferred it; when he could not, he reproduced the censor's alternative. As a result, each early text occasionally preserves profanity excised from the other – and both occasionally reflect a censor's intention, rather than the author's.

'God give 'em joy!' also illustrates the literary significance of Fletcher's profanity. Fletcher might have defended his use of 'the holy Name of God' here on the grounds that it was *not* 'jestingly or profanely' spoken. Even an admired Puritan theologian like William Perkins acknowledged that 'God give you joy' was a 'commendable' salutation.[17] In Fletcher's context, it was particularly appropriate, because the character has just come '*from a wedding*' (1.1.0.2), the wedding of the play's main characters: the widowed Petruccio (based on the wife-taming hero of Shakespeare's play) and Maria (the second wife that Fletcher invented for him). 'Holy matrimony' was – as the prescribed wedding service in the Elizabethan *Book of Common Prayer* insists – 'instituted by God in Paradise . . . signifying unto us the mystical union, that is betwixt Christ and his church: which holy estate Christ adorned and beautified with his presence and first miracle that he wrought in Cana of Galilee, and is commended of Saint Paul to be honourable among all men'. The ceremony ends (as the play begins) with God's blessing on the newly married couple. Fletcher's sympathetic portrayal of 'the disobedience of a wife' (1.2.130), Maria, and of a whole group of women denouncing 'this bane of dull obedience' (2.5.92), cannot be divorced from a wife's wedding vows 'to obey' her husband, and to 'obey him and serve him'. After those vows, every English priest was instructed to quote St Paul's Epistle to the Ephesians: 'Ye Women submit yourselves unto your own husbands as unto the Lord: for the husband is the wife's head even as Christ is the head of the Church . . . Therefore as the church or congregation is subject unto Christ, so likewise let the wives also be in subjection unto their own husbands in all things.' Like the play's blasphemous language, the plot's subversion of the authority of husbands inevitably subverts religious authority. It is no accident that the women's rebellion is compared to a 'new religion' (4.4.167).

Not all the play's uses of the word 'God' are as transparently and immediately related to the sanctity of marriage as 'God give 'em joy!' But a disproportionate amount of the play's profanity is spoken by males reacting to rebellious females. Meg Powers Livingston argues that Herbert's excision of such oaths was calculated to reduce the play's 'subversive' threat. 'In categorizing so much male speech as profane or ribald and then cutting it, Herbert interferes with the male characters' expressions of anxiety, frustration, and hostility, and thereby trivializes the threats posed by the women's behavior.'[18]

Vulgarity and blasphemy thus lead naturally to subversion. In seventeenth-century England (as in twenty-first-century Saudi Arabia and Iran), the authority of fathers and husbands could not be disentangled from the authority of Church and State. Richard Dutton argues that what particularly disturbed Herbert was the play's anti-Catholicism. That sectarian prejudice would not have been objectionable in 1610, but by 1633 it had become much riskier.

Queen Henrietta Maria was openly Roman Catholic, and it wouldn't take too much imagination to connect her to the plot wherein a wife named Maria in a sense *converts* her husband.[19] Indeed, the most extensive cut is a passage in which men who dote on manipulative women are likened to 'Good old Catholics' (3.1.50).

But beyond the specific problem posed by Queen Henrietta Maria loomed larger issues of gender and class. Some critics link the collective female protest that dominates the first half of Fletcher's fiction to very real and disturbing acts of civil disobedience that arose in response to grain shortages and the private enclosure of traditionally common land. In 1633, memory of the Essex food riots of 1622 and 1629 would have still been fresh.[20] Women were involved in at least thirteen anti-enclosure riots during the reign of James I (1603–25), including the famous Midlands riots of 1607; in fact, several of these were 'entirely feminine protests'.[21] In two recorded cases, the female leaders even took on the title of 'Captain', just as Fletcher's Bianca does.[22] Likewise, when Fletcher's 'country wenches' join forces with Maria and other city women, the onstage solidarity of 'city wife' and 'country wife' re-enacts one of the most troubling features of the Midlands riots, when sympathetic citizens of Norfolk trooped out to the countryside to join the 'levellers' who were tearing down new fences and hedges designed to privatize what had previously been public property. Fletcher's patron, the Earl of Huntington, was ordered to suppress the protests and execute all the ringleaders. He was subsequently criticized for being too lenient toward the rebels.[23] Fletcher's play got into trouble with the censors because he, too, was too sympathetic toward a mixed group of urban and rural rebels.

LITERARY HISTORY

In linking Fletcher's dramatization of female rebellion to riots that took place in 1607 we have already moved backward from the censor's writing desk in 1633 to the playwright's writing desk in the first years of James I's reign. *The Tamer Tamed* cannot have been written earlier than the last months of 1609. Many details of the siege, negotiations, and settlement between the men and women echo elements of the 1609 Dutch truce with Spain.[24] Memories of the Midland riots would also have been fresh, and the women's public celebration of the pleasures of eating would have contrasted with the severe food shortages and high prices of 1607–9.[25] Fletcher repeatedly associates the female insurgents with their 'audacious ale' (2.5.41), their daring to 'plant a stand of battering ale' against male authority (2.3.66), their erecting of 'ale-houses' in defiance of courts and constables (2.3.71–3). These and other references to 'noble ale' (2.3.77+2, 2.5.66, 87, 3.2.38, 3.5.11) would have been particularly resonant in the wake of a government proclamation of 12 December 1608 that restricted the manufacture and sale of beer and ale in order to preserve barley, ordering brewers and ale-house keepers to 'make their beer and ale not too strong'.[26] This crackdown immediately led to 'many convictions' – but some local authorities resisted the proclamation, replying that the royal Privy Council 'had no authority to issue such orders', which could be legislated only by Parliament.[27] Once again, Fletcher's fiction echoes the history of political resistance in his own time.

Fletcher's most important source was the real world. Remarriages were as common in early modern London (because of high mortality rates) as in modern America (because of high divorce rates). As it is today, London in 1609 was an international city containing many ethnic communities (with Italian, French, Spanish and Greek names, for instance). Details of the action that may seem unrealistic to modern audiences would have been perfectly familiar in 1609. For instance, Maria's climactic speech at Petruccio's funeral (5.4.17–39) belongs to the widely practised genre of mock epitaph or mock elegy.[28] In 1609 two of Fletcher's friends, Beaumont and Jonson, wrote particularly outrageous mock eulogies for two famous aristocratic women.[29] Fletcher's differs from theirs in being targeted by a woman against a man. But educated professional writers did not have a monopoly on such irreverent responses to real deaths, which were also composed by ordinary (and sometimes even illiterate) survivors.[30] Likewise, in an earlier episode, when Petruccio fakes illness and Maria and others lock him in the house and flee (3.5), their undignified flight would have been immediately recognizable to audiences – and uncomfortably plausible – after an outbreak of plague severe enough to close the London theatres from late July 1608 to early December 1609.[31] Like the fear of AIDS in Tony Kushner's *Angels in America*, the fear of bubonic plague in Fletcher's *Tamer Tamed* reminded audiences that a terminal contagious disease often provokes people to abandon those they claim to love – and that the survivors often forgive those who abandoned them.

In Fletcher's world – as in ours – complete male dominance in marriage was more easily asserted than achieved. This theme links

Fletcher's main plot (where Maria successfully withholds sex on her wedding night) and the subplot (which involves an old man, Moroso, who wants to marry the bride's younger sister, Livia). From the first scene, setting up both plots and the relation between them, Fletcher mocks old Moroso's desire for a young wife, making it perfectly clear that he would never be able to satisfy Livia sexually. Such January–May marriages had been grist for English comedy since Chaucer (one of Fletcher's favourite authors). But Fletcher also emphasizes that Petruccio, if not exactly old, is also not exactly young. Even his friends doubt that this ageing 'dragon' (a widower whose first wife was 'long-since-buried') is 'a fit match' for his 'tender' bride (1.1.7–40). He is an 'old sport' who needs aphrodisiacs to perform on his wedding night (1.1.52–3, 1.3.16–17). When we first see Petruccio, he anticipates doubts about his sexual performance by aggressively laying wagers on it; his buddies jokingly compare him to a 'fearful dwarf', and even he concedes it is 'very possible' he may 'sink' under the pressure of that night's 'business' (1.3.1–33). In the first staged encounter between husband and wife, he again raises the issue: 'I hope you do not doubt I want that mettle / A man should have to keep a woman waking' (1.3.46–7). Bianca calls him an 'old stiff jade,' incapable of learning new tricks (1.3.297–8). In fact, the marriage remains unconsummated throughout the play, and Petruccio is as a result not only exceptionally sexually frustrated but also exceptionally vulnerable to the potential sexual threat posed by other men (his servants, or his friend Sophocles). *The Tamer Tamed* dramatizes, among other things, a second marriage, and a middle-aged man's anxiety about whether he can live up to the macho reputation he acquired when he was younger.

However, Fletcher does not limit his analysis of male insecurity to men marrying younger women. He also satirizes Moroso's younger rival, Roland, whom Livia will ultimately manoeuvre into the marriage bed, despite her father's resistance and Roland's own immaturity. Roland – comically named, as the play reminds us, after the heroic 'Childe Roland' of chivalric myth (2.0.16) – is 'underage' (1.4.54). A mere boy (1.4.57), Roland is too young, as Moroso is too old. Livia's two suitors represent opposite chronological and psychological extremes: Roland as prone to comically excessive, melodramatic, self-pitying despair as Moroso is repeatedly comically victimized by his own self-congratulating, excessive hope. Petruccio should be ideally situated in the middle: mature, determined, experienced but not exhausted. But the best man is also bested.

Fletcher's double plot demonstrates that the problem is not any particular man at any particular age; the problem is marriage. In Fletcher's lifetime Protestant reformers sent Englishmen a mixed message about matrimonial relationships: a wife's 'subjection' to her husband's authority somehow should coexist with her being 'joint governor' of the household.[32] The gap between social expectation and conjugal reality, combined with the demand for incompatible dominance and equality, created a great deal of male anxiety.[33] That anxiety was intensified when a wife defied her husband publicly, thereby endangering his reputation with other men. One of the servants learns of Maria's defiance before her husband does (1.2.197–224); Petruccio first hears of it in male company (1.3.35–98). Maria tells him 'you cannot' (1.3.105) in front of at least five other men, including friends, servants, and his father-in-law. The father-in-law, Petronius, gets even angrier than the husband, in part because a father's reputation was tied to the conduct of his daughters.[34] Throughout the play, the entire male community is affected by, and invested in, Petruccio's contest of wills with his self-assertive wife. This, too, reflects early modern reality: through rituals such as ridings, rough music, and skimmingtons, English communities publicly humiliated husbands who could not control their wives.[35] Every dominated husband set a disturbing precedent for other marriages, threatening the authority and maintenance of traditional hierarchies. For a century after 1560, gender conflict created a 'crisis of order' that extended outward from the household to the whole social fabric.[36]

But if life fed Fletcher's play, so did literature. He took the name, age, nightcaps, and nuptial ambition of Moroso from the character Morose in Ben Jonson's comedy *The Silent Woman* (now better known by its alternative title *Epicene*); Jonson also provided a source for the comic violence against the old man's nose.[37] In Jonson's play, Morose chooses a young bride for her demure silence, then (after he marries her) learns that she is loud, shrill, talkative, bitchy – and not even a woman. Fletcher's 'I never will believe a silent woman; / When they break out they are bonfires' (1.3.110–11) quotes the title of Jonson's play, and refers to the central reversal of its action, marked by Jonson with the astonished question, 'Is this the silent woman?' Another of Jonson's females (this one 'really' a woman) 'has done the miracle of the kingdom', and 'has immortalized herself, with taming of her wild male' (4.3.27–9); likewise, Fletcher's Maria is determined 'to tame Petruccio' her husband

(1.2.108), a feat described as 'a miracle' (1.2.70) that 'will make [her] ever famous' (1.2.195). Fletcher's beleaguered Petruccio is threatened by the prospect of becoming one of Jonson's pathetic married men, who 'is his wife's subject' (2.6.54).

If Fletcher's debt to Jonson is clear, so is the difference between them. In both plays the trouble between bride and groom begins immediately after the wedding. However, Jonson makes the wife's rebellion against her new husband's authority the result of an elaborate hostile conspiracy, planned and managed by men who want revenge on Moroso; the rebellious 'wife' is not just a boy in disguise but a human puppet, who lacks any independent agency. Fletcher, by contrast, repeatedly goes out of his way to emphasize Maria's independence. He also stresses her real love for Petruccio: 'I'd take Petruccio in's shirt . . . Before the best man living' (1.3.102–4). Here and elsewhere, Maria demonstrates that a woman's desire for independence can coexist with heterosexual desire. Jonson's 'silent woman' turns out not to be a woman at all, and Fletcher teases his audience with that possibility:

> *Sophocles.* Call ye this a woman?
> *Petruccio.* Yes, sir, she's a woman.
> *Sophocles.*   Sir, I doubt it.
> (4.4.56–7)

But Petruccio is right: Maria's last words to him are a promise of heterosexual 'pleasure' (5.4.57). Unlike *The Silent Woman*, Fletcher's play does not associate female independence with conspiracy, hatred, hermaphrodites, or a husband desperate enough for divorce to make a public proclamation of his sexual impotence (only to learn that he is no 'husband', she is no 'wife', and no divorce is necessary). *The Tamer Tamed* ends with reiterated, passionate kissing: the consummation desired and expected since the play's first line. God does indeed, in the end, give them joy.

Fletcher also specifically dissociated himself from the elements of Jonson's work that would have offended aristocratic women, like his patroness the Countess of Huntington. We mentioned earlier the scandal caused by Jonson's 1609 epigram, describing Cecilia Bulstrode as a 'Court Pucell' (i.e., 'aristocratic whore'); that scandal was closely followed by the suppression of Jonson's *Silent Woman* because of its alleged offence to Lady Arbella Stuart (in February 1610). Jonson's misogyny was particularly controversial in the very period when *The Tamer Tamed* must have been written and staged.

When Petruccio sarcastically asks Maria if she plans to build 'A college for young scolds' (3.4.86), he echoes the language and the tone of Jonson's play, with its vicious caricature of a 'college' of women who fruitlessly 'toil . . . to *seem* learned' (2.5.57). By contrast to Jonson's collegiates, Fletcher's protagonist Maria is repeatedly called 'learnèd' (1.2.159, 2.2.112, 4.2.106); she demonstrates that learning in her range of classical allusions, which the play never explicitly undercuts or satirizes. Fletcher's appreciative 'she can talk, / God be thanked!' (1.3.121–2) echoes but also inverts Jonson's appalled 'She can talk!' (3.4.49). Jonson's Morose had sought a silent woman; Petruccio, by contrast – like the Earl of Huntington – tells us that he 'married' his wife 'for her wit' (4.1.26).

The play to which *The Tamer Tamed* is most often related is not *The Silent Woman* but Shakespeare's *The Taming of the Shrew*, written almost two decades earlier.[38] Shakespeare's Petruccio, a brash fortune-hunting bachelor, takes on the challenge of wooing the titular 'shrew', the rich but reputedly willful Katherine, who must be brought to subjection in order to serve as a proper wife. As Shakespeare's title suggests, Petruccio achieves his goal, and the play culminates in a 43-line speech whereby Katherine implores her fellow wives to obey their husbands, concluding in a gesture of abject self-abasement: the placing of her hand below her husband's foot. Although George Bernard Shaw, writing in 1897, called the play's final scene 'disgusting to modern sentiments', some recent critics (including some feminists) have argued that Shakespeare's play in fact undermines male supremacy, inviting audiences and readers to 'deconstruct' its apparent pro-patriarchy moral.[39] Such readings say a good deal about an embarrassed modern Shakespeare critical establishment, but it is not clear that they tell us anything about Shakespeare's intentions and audiences' reactions. Who can be better trusted to 'read' Shakespeare's play than one of his contemporaries and sometime collaborators? Working in the small world of early modern London theatre, Fletcher was likelier than a modern critic to know what Shakespeare meant, and he took *The Taming of the Shrew* as meaning just what it said.

The Tamer Tamed; or, The Woman's Prize is, as its double title suggests, a response to two of the most misogynistic plays in the English canon: *The Taming of the Shrew* and *The Silent Woman*. It begins with a speech by Moroso, the character based on Jonson's Morose. But although Jonson's new play was the immediate stimulus, Shakespeare's old play was the softer target, and Fletcher foregrounded his quarrel with *The Taming of the Shrew*. The first act takes place on the wedding day of Shakespeare's Petruccio – widowed after an unspecified number of tumultuous years with Katherine (whose 'taming', we are told, required continual renewal). In contrast to *Shrew*, the first lines of dialogue invite sympathy for Petruccio's bride, Maria, who, according to one male wedding-guest, does not deserve marriage 'to this dragon' (1.1.7). Tranio goes on to say, 'if God had made me woman / And his wife that must be . . . I would . . . spit fire at him' (23–6). The referent of the pronoun 'him' is artfully ambiguous; perhaps it means 'Him'. But if the potential blasphemy of the pronoun can easily be overlooked, the phrase 'if God had made me woman' fairly leaps off the page to a reader familiar with the plays of the period. Shakespeare's gutsier heroines are known to bemoan the limitations of their sex – Beatrice in *Much Ado About Nothing* cries, 'O God that I were a man!' (4.2.308), Lady Macbeth prays to demonic forces to 'unsex' her (*Macbeth* 1.5.40), and Cleopatra ends her life with the stoic exclamation, 'I have nothing / Of woman in me' (*Antony and Cleopatra* 5.2.234–35) – but his male characters invariably endorse conventional gender roles, and they express little if any sympathy for women who transgress.[40] To say 'if I were a woman' would amount to female identification. Such effeminacy is the lot of the boy actor; it makes good comic material for gender-bending fun as in the Epilogue of *As You Like It* (spoken by the boy actor, newly out of drag), but it is not encouraged in adult males, onstage or off.

On the other hand, a certain imaginative cross-dressing is required of a male playwright in penning strong female roles. And it is quite clear whose side Fletcher is on. Tranio's description of what he would do, were he Maria, both predicts and justifies Maria's ensuing rebellion, and the increasingly violent threats thus provoked in the play's central patriarchs – Maria's father and her bridegroom – only serve to strengthen our support for the rebels.

In discussing the sex-strike that dominates the first two acts, critics and editors often invoke Fletcher's apparent classical source – Aristophanes' *Lysistrata*, a play that dramatizes just such a female protest – yet scholars note the parallel without crediting Fletcher's revolutionary use of the device. *The Tamer Tamed* was one of the first English plays based on Aristophanes, and Fletcher one of the first European critics to pay special attention to *Lysistrata*.[41] But Aristophanes' topic is war – that is, political strife in the public male domain. The Greek women strike in order to end a war: in other words, they withhold sex from men in order to stop men from killing one another. At basis, then, the women's rebellion in Aristophanes is designed to benefit the men, even if they are too thuggish to realize this. Fletcher, in wresting the classical sex-strike from its original goal and giving it to women to wield for their *own* benefit, radicalizes the very notion of female collective action. In so doing, he comments on the politics of the private, domestic sphere centuries before the feminist rallying cry that 'the personal is the political'.

Another way in which critics have short-changed Fletcher's originality is in calling the play a 'sequel' to *The Taming of the Shrew*, implying that readers or spectators cannot understand or appreciate *Tamer* without first reading or watching 'part one'. In fact, all the information we need about Petruccio's tempestuous first marriage is laid out in the first few lines of Fletcher's play: his late wife was a 'rebel' who wanted to wear his 'breeches' (1.1.19, 35), and his second wife will have 'no safety' (29) unless she does a better job of gaining the upper hand. One can easily claim that it is the 'prequel' which cannot be read or viewed in isolation, as doing so would lead one to essentialize Shakespeare's attitude toward women as representative of an entire era. Fletcher's play is not a sequel but rather a 'counter-part', as Gerard Langbaine called it in 1691; Langbaine, in the first paragraph of literary criticism devoted to the play, did not subordinate Fletcher to Shakespeare, but simply said that both plays were written 'on the same foundation'.[42] *The Tamer Tamed* was first described as a 'sequel' by the Victorian editor the Reverend Alexander Dyce (who on the same page praised 'the admirable speech of Katherine at the conclusion of *The Taming of the Shrew*').[43] That modern critics prefer 'sequel' says a great deal about their own anxieties and about Shakespeare's formidable place in the canon. In down-playing Fletcher's and Shakespeare's ideological differences, critics save the playwrights from one another and from themselves. This way, Fletcher cannot be accused of disrespecting his elders, and Shakespeare cannot be accused of retrograde sexual politics.

For it all boils down to generational conflict. By the time *Shrew* was first performed, the wife-taming genre was, in fact, past its heyday. And by the time Fletcher posed his challenge, English audiences were ready for a more liberal message; Linda Woodbridge argues that plays produced toward the end of the first decade of the

1600s manifest a kind of backlash against the misogyny of earlier plays.[44] In 1633, when *The Shrew* and *The Tamer* were performed two nights apart, Fletcher's play was the more popular: according to court records, *Shrew* was 'liked' but *Tamer* 'very well liked'.[45]

For critical as well as theatrical purposes, though, much is to be gained by looking at the dialogue between the two taming plays. Beyond the obvious thematic similarities, two common strands of imagery and emphasis come to light: bestial metaphors – required by the misogynist rhetoric that likens women to animals, particularly horses, to be tamed and (sexually) 'ridden' by men – and a concern with basic bodily needs and urges, both the biological/ animal (ingestion, elimination, reproduction) and the specifically human need for clothes.

In the Induction of Shakespeare's play, a nobleman returning with his men from the hunt comes upon a beggar, Christopher Sly, lying dead drunk outside an alehouse. 'O monstrous beast', the lord exclaims, 'how like a swine he lies!' (*Shrew*, Ind.1.32). This sort of invective sets the tone for the play; in the first skirmish between Petruccio and Katherine, the beast-epithets fly: 'ass', 'buzzard', 'turtle', 'wasp', 'cock', 'hen', and 'crab' in the space of 31 lines. In this zoological universe, one measures worth from the dirt upwards.

The nobleman in Shakespeare's Induction is not content to let sleeping beggars lie. The mere sight of Sly's unconscious form moves him to experiment, to 'practise on' him (34). We witness an action committed upon a body that is as low as possible in life, literally and figuratively. The lord proposes: 'What think you: if he were conveyed to bed, / Wrapped in sweet clothes, rings put upon his fingers, / A most delicious banquet by his bed, / And brave attendants near him when he wakes – / Would not the beggar then forget himself?' (35–9). The projected bedding and adornment of Sly, the be-ringing of his fingers, all echo the rites practised upon the body of a bride. 'Believe me', one hunter ruminates over the butt of this lordly practical joke, 'I think he cannot choose' (40). As the old proverb says, 'Beggars should be no choosers' (Tilley B247); nor is this beggar asked to choose. Later in the play we will see two brides essentially prohibited from choosing their mates. Critics have noted the ways Sly and Katherine stand as correlatives and foils. Sly is 'wrapped in sweet clothes', but Kate is promised and denied them; Sly is fed 'a most delicious banquet', but Kate is tantalized by the sight and smell of food and denied it. Like the lord with Sly, Petruccio aims to make the victim 'forget' herself. Whether dressed up or dressed down, feasted or starved, the object of the game endures a reinscription of identity upon and through the surface of the skin.

Then again, Katherine could be worse off. In one of Shakespeare's probable sources, the anonymous ballad *A Merry Jest of a Shrewd and Curst Wife Lapped in Morel's Skin for her Good Behavior*, Petruccio's prototype beats his wife bloody and then stuffs her into the salted skin of his dead horse, Morel. Presumably, it would not be enough to strip her of her velvet cap or dress, for that would leave her the dignity of her human skin. As critics and editors are quick to point out, Shakespeare's protagonist seems far more humane by contrast, choosing simply to beat the tailor while his wife looks on and to send away her new dress.[46] He needs no horse-hide to prove his point, having just declared her, 'My horse, my ox, my ass, my any thing' (3.3.104).

From Sly's 'sweet clothes' to Morel's skin, clothing in these tales becomes a second skin, to be relished or disrelished at a deeply psychological level. Petruccio himself partakes in the masquerade he enforces upon his bride, arriving in tatters for his wedding ceremony. A wedding-guest berates him for coming 'hither so *unlike himself*' (3.2.104; emphasis added), a statement that reminds us of Sly's 'forget[ting] himself', bedazzled by his new clothes. Petruccio makes the excuse, 'To me she's married, not unto my clothes.' Yet in the 1590s, when sumptuary laws still forbade literal dressing-up – that is, dressing above one's social station – this discrepancy between real worth and mere apparel was far from obvious. Petruccio's dressing-down is frowned upon precisely because it permits someone like Sly to dress up – and not think it a 'flatt'ring dream'.

Petruccio does make a case for his defiance of sumptuary norms, asking rhetorically whether 'the jay [is] more precious than the lark' or 'the adder better than the eel' because of its 'painted skin' (4.3.173–6). These analogies seem innocuous enough: snakes and birds are species that may shed or moult, seemingly painlessly. But when tallying up the animal references in the text, the creature that steps forth is not armoured with feathers or scales: the word 'horse' occurs twenty-four times, upstaging even the play's rodent namesake.[47] Shakespeare's text bears the markings – one might say, the hoof-prints – of poor Morel, Katherine's flayed fellow mammal. Peel off the painted skin of Petruccio's rhetoric and you find, beneath, the old, pickled skin of misogyny.

So how is Katherine to save her hide? By submitting. Another term for taming is 'breaking', a term bandied about after

Katherine's ill-fated music lesson: her tutor tries to 'break her to the lute', in return for which 'she hath broke the lute to' him (2.1.147–8). The slapstick humour of Katherine's 'breaking' her tutor's head relies on our consciousness of the discrepancy between real and figurative violence: by casting the male act of 'breaking' as figurative and benign (a mere music lesson) and the female violence as real, Shakespeare obscures the threat of violence inherent in the very notion of wife-taming. For to 'break' a wild horse, to 'break' its will, one must literally break its hide. And once the animal is tamed it must still be trained – this gentler procedure involving a combination of punishment *and* reward. When it's all over, the beast will (as Petruccio puts it) 'know her keeper's call' (4.1.194) and may even eat an apple out of his hand. In the last scene of Shakespeare's play, Katherine comes when she is called, and takes her reward in an off-stage bed.

Fortunately for feminism, Katherine has her revenge, albeit posthumously, in Fletcher's rebuttal. Petruccio's second wife concludes their wedding day barricaded in her upstairs chamber, refusing to consummate the marriage until her notorious shrew-tamer husband comes to her 'tame as fear' (*Tamer Tamed*, 1.2.114). This rebellion is supported by her cousin Bianca, seemingly drawn from Shakespeare's character of the same name, Katherine's initially passive but ultimately 'shrewish' sister (her docile demeanour being presented as a strategic sham, which she discarded once she was married). Fletcher implies that Bianca is Petruccio's ex-sister-in-law, and her vindication of Katherine manifests another ideological contrast with Shakespeare's play, wherein the 'good' sister and the 'bad' were pitted against one another so successfully that they never recognized their mutual enemy in patriarchal power. Female solidarity in Fletcher's play, however, is not limited to Bianca and Maria (or, posthumously, Bianca and Katherine). Unlike Katherine – isolated in life as in her protest against male domination – Fletcher's heroine gathers a troupe of female companions who stock up her room with food and wine and stand guard against male intrusion into their stronghold. Maria declares,

> By the faith I have
> In my own noble will, that childish woman
> That lives a prisoner to her husband's pleasure
> Has lost her making, and becomes a beast
> Created for his use, not fellowship.
>
> (1.2.137–41)

One of her consorts responds, 'Why then, let's all wear breeches' (1.2.147). So the shrews don breeches and the battle ensues, with the men below on the main stage, bewildered and chagrined, and the women above, loudly defiant. As in the window sequence in *Romeo and Juliet*, the upper stage here delineates an off-limits female world, but this time the context is siege warfare, not wooing. Reinforcements arrive, 'led by a tanner's wife' who (the men say) 'flayed her husband in her youth, and made / Reins of his hide to ride the parish' (2.3.42–5). These women turn 'Morel's Skin' inside-out.

Or rather, upside-down. Fletcher repeatedly takes up Shakespeare's equestrian metaphors, but puts the woman 'on top', casting her as the rider. 'I am ridden', the love-struck Roland complains of his mistress Livia, 'And spur-galled to the life of patience' (2.2.23–4). Roland himself calls the old Moroso 'bobtail jade' and (sarcastically) 'stallion' (1.4.41, 44). Bianca compares Petruccio to the Trojan horse, that 'wooden jade' (2.2.31–2), and Maria urges him to be a 'courser' rather than a 'jade' (4.4.171). In one of the funniest bits of ribaldry, two men look on slack-jawed while Maria arranges to buy 'a great-horse' or stallion, perhaps not to be ridden 'with a side-saddle' (3.3.70). 'Have a care', she orders the horseman, 'He be an easy doer' (73). Interestingly, the play's most violent riding image is directed at a man: may 'The fiend ride through him booted and spurred, with a scythe at's back,' one man curses another (5.2.67).

True, when men use these tropes, they more frequently gender the mount as female, and references to the women as jades, fillies, and colts (1.2.59, 161–2; 1.4.17–18; 2.5.12, 125; 5.4.87–8) slightly outnumber the overt inversions mentioned above. But the fact that Fletcher even imagines the woman 'on top' – sexually, figuratively, or (as in the staging of the sex-strike) spatially – manifests his radical vision.[48] By contrast, Shakespeare's play only twists the horse-and-rider metaphor once – and that is to put the *horse* on top of its female *rider*, Katherine. Petruccio's servant delivers a purportedly comic anecdote about an offstage mishap wherein the bride's 'horse fell and she under her horse' in a quagmire and 'she was bemoiled' (*Shrew* 3.3.65–8).

It is the men who get 'bemoiled' in Fletcher's play. One of the most effective weapons employed by the besieged women is the 'charged' or loaded chamber-pot. Likewise Livia humiliates her old dotard suitor by giving him 'purging comfits . . . That spoiled his camlet breeches' (5.1.82–4). Images of women as 'leaky vessels' were

standard in early modern medical and literary texts, but Fletcher's
men leak at least as much as his women.[49] Both young Roland and
his elderly rival Moroso cry copiously when Livia feigns illness;
when Roland loses a wager by going back to his beloved, he feels
'an hundred pound / Running directly from' him as though he
'pissed it' (65–6). Scatological humour can even target men in
otherwise viciously misogynistic male speech, as when an (allegedly)
drunken country woman is described as 'belch[ing] out . . .
courtship' that gives its object 'twenty stools' (3.2.38–9). The point
may be that the old woman's courtship is so repulsive – or fright-
ening – as to give the poor man the runs, but here the more embar-
rassing incontinence is male.

The biological equalities of Fletcher's play are linked to its
overturning of gendered hierarchies. That bottoms-up logic is part
and parcel of what Mikhail Bakhtin terms the 'carnivalesque'.[50] The
same is true, of course, of the play's interest in food, feasting, and
revelry. Though the women's cause is serious and their rhetoric
martial, essentially they protest by *having fun*. So as not to become
'prisoner[s] to [men's] pleasure', they create a sanctuary for their
own pleasure, meanwhile arming themselves against unwanted male
ingress. In memory of the ill-dressed, ill-fed Katherine, the rebels
demand money for fine clothes, gorge on pudding and pork, and
drink, and drink, and drink, and drink.

So as not to dismiss as misogynist parody these scenes of female
indulgence, we recall the way in which the opening of the play estab-
lishes sympathy for Maria, who 'must . . . not eat, / Drink, . . . piss,
/ Unless [Petruccio] bid her', and whom he may even 'bury' within
'three weeks' (1.1.45–8). When Maria decides to protest, she is asked
whether she has 'a stomach to it' (1.2.63). She does, for she must,
in order to fill her stomach and keep her bones in flesh. This is far
from the traditional female bodily protest epitomized by the hunger-
strike which killed Lady Arbella Stuart.[51] But the stakes are just as
high here: Petruccio, for instance, immediately threatens to 'starve
'em out' (1.3.278).

By adding a festive element to the women's rebellion, Fletcher
undermines any sense that female independence is opposed to pleasure. Maria's sexual withholding cannot be reduced to an affirma-
tion of the cult of virginity. On the contrary, when Petruccio
threatens to ease his sexual frustrations with her chambermaid,
Maria threatens to do the same with his own butler. Petruccio
admits that, before their wedding, she'd shown no signs of sexual

reticence, but 'would shower / Her kisses so upon' him (3.3.39–40).
For Maria, bodily integrity does not come at the expense of bodily
pleasure; in fact, she becomes a vocal advocate for not just her own
but every woman's right to a fulfilling sex-life. Contemplating Livia's
prospective marriage with old Moroso, she opines: 'What a grief of
heart is't . . . to rise sport-starved!' (1.2.82–5).

The radical nature of the women's anti-hunger strike is under-
scored by the violence of the men's response to it. Maria's father
Petronius vows to 'see all passages stopped', and Petruccio takes the
metaphor and runs with it:

> Let's in, and each provide him to his tackle.
> We'll fire 'em out, or make 'em take their pardons –
> Hear what I say – on their bare knees.
>
> (1.3.286–8)

In the martial/sexual language of the men, the barricaded bridal
chamber metonomizes the virginal body within. And as the conjugal antagonism intensifies, the male threats grow increasingly
visceral:

> *Petronius.* Give her a crab-tree cudgel.
> *Petruccio.*   So I will,
>   And after it a flock-bed for her bones,
>   And hard eggs, till they brace her like a drum.
>   . . .
>   She shall not know a stool in ten months, gentlemen.
>
> (2.3.28–32)

Petruccio would suit the punishment to the crime: his wife seals
herself from his sexual entry, so he threatens to seal her up anally.
And as to her female cohorts, 'They swarm like wasps, and nothing
can destroy 'em / But stopping of their hive and smothering of 'em'
(35–6).

Despite the men's complaints about the women's 'extremely
fearful' garrulity, and despite the all-too-familiar comparisons of
female tongues with weapons (1.3.57–98), it is male speech that is
infused with aggression.[52] In a moment of climactic rage, Petruccio
prays for patience, so as not to make Maria an 'example / By . . .
flaying her, / Boiling, or making verjuice, drying her' (3.3.43–5).
Perhaps we might give the hero some credit, here, for self-restraint.
But, as the saying goes, there is more than one way to skin a cat.
The husband in 'Morel's Skin', for instance, need only flay his *horse*;

his wife knows that she is next in line, so the threat is obvious. Likewise, Shakespeare's Petruccio need not lay a finger on Katherine in order to get (so to speak) under her skin. The cold house, the scanty food, and the shabby clothes alone might suffice; add his violence toward the servants (clearly an indirect threat), his sun-is-the-moon mind-games, and his nicknaming her, and we have all the necessary elements for dehumanization. Emily Detmer even suggests – in a 'strategically anachronistic' feminist reading – that these tactics and Katherine's response to them closely resemble what we now call Stockholm Syndrome.[53]

Such brutality may seem a far cry from the dressing-up gag of Shakespeare's Induction. But perhaps not. Without our clothes, humankind becomes, in the words of Shakespeare's Lear, a 'poor, bare, forked animal' (3.4.101–2) – not just an animal but a naked one, defenceless against the elements. In light of the above observations, the trick played on Sly – and its corollary in the treatment of Katherine – appear increasingly insidious. The very notion that a suit of clothes can make a man forget himself carries with it the assumption that clothes make the self, and therefore can mar it as easily.

The attack on female adornment has been treated as one of misogyny's more trivial cruelties. Fletcher may not have agreed: he died of the plague, in 1625, because he stayed in London a few days, waiting for a new suit of clothes from his tailor. A man who risks his life for a new outfit is not likely to despise women for their interest in clothes. Clothing defines not only the aristocratic self, but also the human self, and finally, even the living self; this second skin is vulnerable indeed. When Katherine throws off and tramples her hat at Petruccio's bidding, she is truly tamed. And Fletcher's play, by equating this husbandly caprice with the threat of starvation, penetration, smothering, and flaying, exposes the latent violence in Petruccio's circus-trick, the threat of violence required to tame anything, human or not. Taming a wife means not only reducing her to an animal but reducing her to an animal in fear for its life.

In contrast to Katherine's craven performance, Fletcher's female rebels perform their own celebratory strip-tease: in the safety of their upstairs room, they 'dance with their coats tucked up to their bare breeches, / And bid the kingdom kiss 'em' (2.5.39–40). Like their defiant feasting, this is a serious bit of fun, whose comic effect should not obscure its revolutionary bent. The fact that Fletcher equates bared breeches and bared bums only reiterates our close ties with our clothes, underscoring the danger and potency of this bare-faced insult to the male power structure. It is with triumph that Maria demands, and gets, 'fourteen yards of satin', 'Another suit of horses', and 'ten cast of hawks' (3.3.61–6) when the siege is over.

A shrew is a rodent – that is, a small furry animal with sharp teeth and claws that it might easily turn on 'the hand that feeds' it. Rather than submitting to petting or feeding, Fletcher's women feed, feast, themselves. And their oral exuberance, manifested vocally and gastronomically, makes the play a pleasure on more than political grounds. To sum up: we might, with a nod to Patricia Parker's paradigm in *Literary Fat Ladies*, call *Shrew* a skinny play and *Tamer* a fat one – a stylistic (and gendered) contrast that holds regardless of where we place Shakespeare's intentions.[54] Feminist scholars from Caroline Walker Bynum to Susan Bordo have stressed the crucial role of food and flesh in writings by and about women.[55] And there is, as Bakhtin argues, a certain ethic of fatness in Renaissance literature, traces of a folk tradition that celebrates the flesh in its generative function. This is the ethic of carnival, a world of popular rebellion, a world of bodily excess and renewal, a world ecstatically upside-down.

The women in *The Tamer Tamed* do turn their world upside-down when they march up to Maria's chamber, bar the door, and tell the kingdom, in effect, 'Kiss my arse.' Women are seen as lower in the chain of being, closer to the dirt, but these women do not wait, like Christopher Sly, for someone to 'take [them] up'. True to the spirit of carnival, they assert themselves bodily, and in doing so they burst Petruccio's patriarchal bubble. In context, Maria's statement 'I have tamed ye, / And now am vowed your servant' (5.4.44–5) is not a capitulation but a truce. After all, in this scene she brings him to feel so *low* as to lay down and feign death, a comic inversion of the first scene's prediction that 'he will bury her . . . within . . . three weeks' (1.1.47–8). And in case there is still any doubt about Fletcher's moral, the Epilogue tells us that the play means 'To teach both sexes due equality' (5.4.97).

One seventeenth-century reader of Fletcher who took this lesson seriously was Margaret Cavendish, Duchess of Newcastle. *The Tamer Tamed* clearly inspired elements of her closet drama *The Convent of Pleasure* (1668), in which one Lady Happy forswears marriage because husbands 'make the Female sex their slaves'. She uses her fortune to erect a lavish, all-female separatist community, whose yard-thick walls enclose cultivated parklands, orchards, gardens, and every possible luxury:

> We'll clothe ourselves with softest silk
> And linen fine, as white as milk.
> We'll please our sight with pictures rare,
> Our nostrils with perfumèd air,
> Our ears with sweet melodious sound
> Whose substance can nowhere be found,
> Our taste with sweet delicious meat
> And savoury sauces we will eat.

As a cloister dedicated not to Christian piety but female sensory pleasure, the 'convent' resembles the sanctified female space of Maria's chamber in *Tamer Tamed*. Though Lady Happy insists that her female utopia proffers only the *chaste* pleasures derived from feasting, music, and art, some of the convent's activities bear a striking resemblance to Maria's bacchanalia with its breech-baring female captains and 'firking' of fiddles. Lady Happy's comrades, for instance, entertain themselves in cross-dressed courtship rituals whereby women woo other women. It is this diversion which, in fact, leads to Lady Happy's downfall – and that of her happy community – when a prince dons female disguise, infiltrates the convent, and wins her seemingly lesbian love. This ruse appears in the text as an alternative to the proposed storming of the convent, which strongly echoes Fletcher's play: 'Let's every one carry a firebrand to fire it', one man, Petruccio-like, urges the others; he is answered, in still more Fletcherian echoes, 'Yes, and smoke them out, as they do a swarm of bees.' (Compare 1.3.279–87, 2.3.35.) But, as in *Tamer Tamed*, these violent proposals come to nothing: the men forgo the option of siege against so strongly fortified an edifice, instead proposing to disguise themselves as 'lusty country wenches . . . Dairy maids, and the like', thereby replicating the cross-class female community staged by Fletcher. Ultimately, though, Lady Happy's undoer disguises himself as a princess; once he is unveiled, it is his princely prerogative that allows him to claim her. Cursorily asking the permission of his counsellors – not the bride herself – he threatens to 'have her by force of arms' in the face of any objections. In an eerily defeatist moment in what might otherwise be called utopian fantasy, the vibrant, independent, visionary heroine passes in silence from the text. Whether this constitutes Cavendish's pessimistic reading of Maria's 'I have tamed thee, and now am vowed thy servant', or the author's personal gesture of feminist despair, the Fletcher–Cavendish connections manifest the provocative force of *The Tamed Tamed*.

Margaret Cavendish admired many of Shakespeare's plays, and specifically praised his Cleopatra, Anne Page, Mistress Page, Mistress Ford, Beatrice, Mistress Quickly, and Doll Tearsheet; but she never praised *The Taming of the Shrew* or its female characters.[56] Whether or not we can excuse Shakespeare's politics in *Shrew* on the basis of his being 'a man of his time' (a claim frequently voiced by the same critics who elsewhere praise him as 'universal'), it was Fletcher's reply to Shakespeare that inspired Cavendish. Sadly, it remains revolutionary today.

STAGE HISTORY

The Tamer Tamed was probably first performed between December 1609 and April 1610 in the Whitefriars Theatre by the Children of the Queen's Revels.[57] This was the same venue and company responsible for Jonson's *The Silent Woman*. The Whitefriars was, like the Blackfriars, a fashionable indoor playing space, with smaller audiences, more expensive seats, and a more intimate acting style than outdoor arenas such as the Globe.[58] The Whitefriars was also the first 'West End' theatre, in the area between the City of London and Westminster.[59] Its location and amenities tended to attract a relatively well-educated, well-to-do audience. Like other indoor theatres, it divided plays into five acts, with musical interludes between them.[60] Those intervals would have shaped the rhythm of performance and the audience's perception of the play's structure. Act 1 ends with first Maria and then Livia having publicly and physically embarrassed their suitors; Act 2, with the men's surrender to the women's conditions; Act 3, with Petruccio alone on stage, after Maria has persuaded all his male friends to abandon him; Act 4, with Petruccio departing for France, after Maria turns the table on his threat to leave her. The sequence of pauses in the performance elegantly mapped and emphasized Maria's conquest of physical and social space, and the play's movement from a physical and public struggle to a more private, psychological contest of wills.[61] Having been defeated, isolated, and exiled, the only thing left for Petruccio is death – which Act 5 supplies, confirming Maria's control not only of space but of time, as she demonstrates her ability to shape how others will remember him.

When the King's Men performed *The Taming of the Shrew*, the male parts would have been played by adult males, and the female parts by boys or adolescents; when the Queen's Revels company performed *The Tamer Tamed*, all the parts would have been played by boys or 'youths'. As a result, the Whitefriars company could perform plays with more female characters – and with longer and more complicated female roles. Maria speaks 4193 words, Bianca 2026, and Livia 1702; altogether, women characters speak more than 38 per cent of our edited text (which we believe represents the script performed in Fletcher's lifetime). Moreover, the young men who played adult males would have needed to wear artificial beards. Full beards were not only the universal sign of manhood in the period but were also individualized in colour, thickness, and cut; as a result, children's companies used an extraordinary number and variety of costume beards.[62] In the first performances of *The Tamer Tamed* the sexes in contention were equally matched and equally artificial: the femme-effect produced by prosthetic breasts, wigs, and white make-up, the man-effect produced by prosthetic beards, codpieces, and ruddy or brown make-up. Masculinity was as fragile, as much a matter of consciously artificial role-playing, as femininity.

We do not know how audiences responded to those first performances. But from about 1609 to about 1690 the plays written or co-written by Fletcher were more popular than those of any other playwright (including Shakespeare).[63] When Fletcher died in 1625, John Ford's elegy proclaimed 'that from his pen Men formed a language, and that language men'. Fletcher's style, 'the quick marriage of his rich conceits', simultaneously 'copious and refined', exemplifying the 'familiar use of master words', taught 'the court . . . to speak, the schools to write'. Ford did not single out *The Tamer Tamed* – or any other play – because 'who of his likes any, must like all'.[64] *The Tamer Tamed* belonged to a body of work that, for most of the seventeenth century, was celebrated as an aesthetically coherent canon.

After Fletcher's death, *The Tamer Tamed* was extensively censored and successfully revived in 1633. The censor's intervention made its gender politics less threatening; so, less obviously, did its performance by the King's Men. First, they commissioned a new prologue.[65]

Ladies to you, in whose defence and right
Fletcher's brave muse prepared herself to fight

A battle without blood – 'twas well fought too;
The victory's yours, though got with much ado –
We do present this comedy, in which
A rivulet of pure wit flows, strong and rich
In fancy, language, and all parts that may
Add grace and ornament to a merry play,
Which this may prove. Yet not to go too far
In promises, from this our female war
We do intreat the angry men would not
Expect the mazes of a subtle plot,
Set speeches, high expressions, and – what's worse
In a true comedy – politic discourse.
The end we aim at is to make you sport,
Yet neither gall the city nor the court.
Hear and observe his comic strain, and when
You're sick of melancholy, see't again.
'Tis no dear physic, since 'twill quite the cost –
Or his intentions, with our pains, are lost.

This prologue emphasizes the play's cleverness ('wit'), imagination ('fancy'), and style ('language'). But it also defines 'comedy' as mere 'sport', a therapeutic cure for depression ('melancholy'), without any larger political or satirical ambitions. This message reinforces the censor's work in de-politicizing and trivializing the play. The new prologue also reinforces old gender stereotypes and divisions: a play that pleases women will not satisfy men, because it will not provide the more ambitious material that men expect (a complicated plot, long speeches like those found in classical tragedy, sublime language, and serious political analysis). A play associated with women cannot provide more than 'grace and ornament', like women themselves a temporary but pleasant diversion from serious male business.

More subtly, by pairing Fletcher's play with *The Taming of the Shrew* instead of *The Silent Woman* (or *Lysistrata*), the King's Men silently redefined the terms for its interpretation. Moreover, although Maria, Bianca, and Livia continued to be played by boy actors, the men's roles were transferred to adult actors, who physically and professionally dominated the apprentices who represented women. Artificiality and performance anxiety were no longer evenly distributed across genders; the men were veterans with a mastery and self-assurance their younger underlings could not match. This hierarchical theatrical division between male and female characters was, of course, taken even further after the Restoration, when actresses replaced boy actors.

The Tamer Tamed was in fact one of the first plays performed after the return of Charles II and the official re-opening of the theatres. 'The Tamer Tamed – what do the Players mean?' asked Thomas Jordan's prologue for a performance on 23 June 1660. 'Shall we have Rump and Rebel in the Scene?' The scatological challenge to patriarchal authority was inevitably correlated with other forms of rebellion (the 'Rump' Parliament and the 'Great Rebellion' of the 1640s). But like the 1633 prologue, the 1660 prologue made a pre-emptive strike against the play's larger implications, reassuring the audience that 'This Play, *The Tamer tam'd*, is Fletcher's wit – / A man that pleased all palates; therefore sit / And see'.[66] Audiences apparently liked what they saw, because the play continued to be revived. Thomas Betterton, who quickly established himself as the greatest of Restoration actors, had a 'considerable role' in it, and the company also included Edward Kynaston, the last famous transvestite player of female roles. Samuel Pepys saw a 'very fine play called *The Tamer Tamed*, very well acted' at the Cockpit in Drury Lane on 30 October 1660, and he saw it again, 'well done' by a different company at the Theatre Royal on 31 July 1661.[67] It also played at the Red Bull in 1660, and another performance is recorded on 23 December 1661. It was performed before Charles II twice, once at court in 1668 and again in a public theatre in 1674.[68]

None of these Restoration performances was linked with Shakespeare's *The Taming of the Shrew*, which does not seem to have been in the repertoire at all until April 1667, when the comedian John Lacy adapted it as *Sauny the Scot*. That adaptation, first printed in 1698, concludes with a speech by Petruccio: 'I've *Tamed the Shrew*, but will not be ashamed / If next you see the very *Tamer Tamed*.' Whereas in the late twentieth century the popularity of Shakespeare's play led to revivals of Fletcher's, in the late seventeenth century it apparently worked the other way around, the success of *Tamer* leading to an attempt to revive *Taming* (which however required heavy adaptation to make it palatable). Lacy's adaptation of Shakespeare's play may have been regularly piggy-backed with *Tamer* in the 1660s and 1670s.[69]

Tamer did not appeal to the more conventional bourgeois tastes of the last decades of the seventeenth century, and after Jeremy Collier's 1698 attack on 'the Profaneness and Immorality of the English Stage' it became increasingly difficult to stage any of

Fletcher's work. David Garrick adapted the play as an afterpiece, eliminating the Livia plot; it was performed at least three times, twice in 1757 and once in 1760, with the famous Hannah Pritchard playing Maria. She spoke the new epilogue 'in the Character of Maria'.

> Well! since I've thus succeeded in my plan,
> And conquered this all-conquering tyrant, man,
> To farther conquests still my soul aspires,
> And all my bosom glows with martial fires.[70]

Unlike any of the seventeenth-century performances, this revival was performed in the middle of a long war (the Seven Years' War against the French, the first truly global war); it thus placed the conceit of a female army in a social context that resembled the original circumstances of Aristotle's *Lysistrata* more than those of Fletcher's *Tamer Tamed*. But the 1760 prologue does not oppose female peace to male war. Instead, Hannah Pritchard's Maria resolves that 'these brave lads should be assisted', and elaborates a plan for a 'variegated army' of women to conquer India ('Temples of gold, and diamond mines we'll rob') and America (because women are even better than Indians when it comes 'To art, disguise, and strategem').

The play did not reappear in theatres until the twentieth century, a victim of the dual forces of increasing English prudishness about Flecther's bawdy and the Romantics' deification of Shakespeare – and Shakespeare alone – as the national poet. (These two factors are not necessarily unrelated.) It is surely no accident that the first modern revival of *The Tamer Tamed* took place on the heels of the feminist movement. That performance in 1979 opened the short-lived Harbor Shakespeare Festival in Baltimore, Maryland; reviews were mixed, but most complaints were about long speeches that inexperienced actors did not know what to do with. This was followed, over the next two decades, by a handful of minor, poorly documented productions (all outside England).[71] Given this scanty performance history, and the contrasting over-production of Shakespeare's *Shrew* all the while, it was not surprising that the first millennial revival took the credit for being the first production since the Restoration. This adaptation, at the Arcola Theater in London in 2001, called itself 'Shrew'd: The Taming of the Shrew and the Tamer Tamed', and comprised a hybrid of both plays, each pared down to just over an hour's playing time. Reviews were quite enthusiastic,

with at least one critic wondering why *Tamer* had been so
neglected.[72] This set the precedent for the Royal Shakespeare
Company's 2003 production of a full-length *Tamer Tamed* alongside
Shrew, using the same cast.

This double-feature deserves some attention, as it represents the
rich theatrical potential of Fletcher's play, either in dialogue with
Shakespeare's or on its own. The *Shrew* production did its best
to play the text 'straight', but added much stage action to make
Katherine really seem to need taming. As feminist critics and
actresses have pointed out, despite Katherine's reputation as 'an
irksome, brawling scold' (*Shrew* 1.2.186), she in fact says very little
until her final speech, and there is no evidence that she raises her
voice on stage.[73] In an age when women were exhorted to be 'chaste,
silent, and obedient', speaking out of turn at all would warrant
labelling as a scold, with all the attendant metaphors likening
tongues to weapons and complaints to 'loud 'larums' (*Shrew*
1.2.205). In Gregory Doran's interpretation, Katherine became a
howling, stomping, door-slamming hellion. At the same time, Doran
exaggerated Petruccio's vices. Michael Billington describes Jasper
Britton's character as 'a nervy, self-hating psychotic in deep shock
over his father's death'. Together with Alexandra Gilbreath's wild-
eyed, 'paternally-abused Kate', the two make 'a damaged couple
finding mutual support'.[74] The final speech was played sincerely –
and somewhat sadly. Then, in the 'sequel' we saw the same actress
transformed into the feisty and resourceful Maria, continually out-
smarting the same blustering and not-too-bright Petruccio. The production did justice to *Tamer*'s carnivalesque atmosphere, most
notably by bringing the 'breeches dance' onstage, rather than having
the men hear the women singing 'within'. Staged this way, the song
became a splendid gesture not just of female defiance, but of female
celebration and solidarity: the women linked arms and danced in a
circle, beating an infectious rhythm with their clogs. Audience
members exited humming the tune.

Reviews of the double-billing were uniformly enthusiastic, and
even the diehard bardophiles found Fletcher's play irresistible.
Indeed, the occasional barb at the expense of 'the lesser play-wright'
rings a hollow note; when a preference for Shakespeare's play is
announced, the complaints against Fletcher are vague. Most reviews
of *Tamer Tamed* in particular convey responses of delight and reve-
lation. Kate Bassett called the play 'a proto-feminist gem', praising
Gilbreath's Maria and her 'merry insurrection. The dialogue is pep-

pered with explosively funny jokes and the cast's exuberance is a joy.'[75] Charles Spencer raved, 'The comedy storms on to the stage as a wonderfully exhilarating proto-feminist piece, combining outrageous humour with rich humanity and good sense.'[76] Some critics waxed irreverent: 'Shakespeare's worst play and its lesser known sequel prove an inspired coupling' reads Susannah Clapp's subheadline. She went on to write, 'Suddenly the RSC looks as if it has got a point again', and praised *Tamer* as 'a welcome stand against gigantism' and as 'full-throttle comedy with unswerving intent'. Clapp saw the 'glorious' clog-dance as epitomizing the 'glee' of the production. Her relief at the rebuttal of Shakespeare is almost palpable: 'Seen as only one side of an argument, Shakespeare's most wretched play (a play I thought I never wanted to see again) becomes more airy and infinitely more interesting.'[77]

The success of the RSC production almost immediately inspired other Shakespeare festivals to consider staging *Tamer Tamed*. At the very least, it provides a solution to the directorial dilemma of how to approach Shakespeare's problem play, de-necessitating such post-obedience-speech gags as Katherine's winking at the audience or (a particularly desperate move) her stripping down to a black leather body-suit and riding offstage on a Harley Davidson. Indeed, Doran confessed that he could not have staged *Shrew* without *Tamer* alongside it; this 'takes the pressure off' the director, who would otherwise feel compelled to soften *Shrew's* misogyny.[78] In the final analysis, however, Fletcher's play stands on its own as a work of art.

CRITICAL HISTORY

Fletcher was, without doubt, enormously esteemed in his own time, and was by all objective measures more successful as a dramatist than his senior contemporary, Shakespeare. Most often associated with Beaumont, he none the less could hold his own in sole authored works such as *Tamer Tamed* (indeed, of the fifty-two plays attributed to both authors, no more than twelve are, technically speaking, collaborations between them). Even so, the 1647 publication of the Folio of *The Comedies and Tragedies of Beaumont and Fletcher* solidified the two names as the most prominent and popular literary partnership in the century. Their reputations, however, suffered greatly in the eighteenth and nineteenth centuries, when editors of their plays felt compelled to make excuses for or even to censor their bawdy language. The preface of the 1750 edition states, 'It is necessary to apologize for a fault which must shock every modest Reader: It is their frequent use of *gross* and *indecent* Expressions.' The editor goes on to observe that such 'Grossness does not occur quite so often in' Shakespeare, and explains that he would have excised these 'indecencies' had it not been for the pressure of the book-sellers.[79] The problem continued into the next century, exacerbated by Victorian prudery. Leigh Hunt's 1855 edition of the 'selected' plays of Beaumont and Fletcher complains that the authors 'degrade love by confining it to the animal passion', anticipating the worst of 'Rochester' (presumably for obscenity) and 'Swift' (presumably for scatalogy). By this point, the reputation of the once-famous literary partnership has waned to the point where the famous essayist, who had championed the work of Keats, Shelley, and Byron, can say that Beaumont and Fletcher 'are authors destined to survive only in frag- ments'.[80] Notably, although Hunt found something to quote from forty-eight plays, *Tamer Tamed* was not among them. Finally, by 1887, critics felt compelled to justify *any* edition of Beaumont and Fletcher, even a selection of their best plays (which did not include *Tamer Tamed*, and indeed omitted it from the list of their works). In his introduction the now-forgotten poet and novelist J. S. Fletcher identified 'The most marked characteristic of Beaumont and Fletcher's work' as 'a terrible grossness of thought and expression'. This is followed by six pages agonizing over the indecency problem. 'The songs scattered through these pages are equal, I think, to any- thing which Shakespeare gave us in the way of lyrics.' Had their work 'been purged of its unfortunate looseness of expression', the editor wonders, 'is it too much to affirm that it would have proved of an *almost* equal order of merit with the writings of their great contemporary?'[81]

That 'almost' is telling, and touches on another crucial concern for eighteenth- and nineteenth-century scholars: Fletcher's rela- tionship with the older dramatist. In particular, scholars fretted over the seeming irreverence of Beaumont and Fletcher's occasional Shakespearean allusions, for instance, Petruccio's flabbergasted, 'Something I'll do / But what it is, I know not' (2.3.85), which, according to one editor, seemed to 'ridicule' King Lear.[82] Other scholars took pains to defend Beaumont and Fletcher from the charge of 'sneer[ing]' at Shakespeare.[83] Still, the reputation of the pair – and hence of Fletcher alone – could not survive the rampant bardolatry of the nineteenth century.[84] 'Every good Author pleases more', an eighteenth-century editor acknowledged, 'the more he is examined; (hence perhaps that Partiality of Editors to their own Authors; by a more intimate Acquaintance, they discover more of their Beauties than they do of others).'[85] This editor was talking, in 1750, about the 'beauties' of Beaumont and Fletcher, but his statement ironically anticipates the overwhelming partiality of male scholars for Shakespeare, a partiality which, because self-perpetuating (both textual editing and textual criticism being *competitive* practices), created a veritable intellectual vortex, lasting the better part of three centuries.

The logic of bardolatry typically deifies one writer by demonizing others.[86] This logic also encourages critics to totalize authors, setting a generality called 'Shakespeare' against another generality called 'Beaumont-and-Fletcher'. Such binary oppositions usually collapse under objective scrutiny: both Shakespeare and Fletcher wrote more than thirty plays over the course of more than two decades in the constantly changing world of theatrical fashion, and both often collaborated with other playwrights. We might agree that *Antony and Cleopatra* is a greater play than any of Fletcher's tragedies, without assuming that everything Shakespeare wrote is better than anything Fletcher did. Criticism can produce more reliable – and more fruitful – results by comparing individual plays than whole canons. *Tamer Tamed* explicitly invites us to do just that. But even then, Fletcher complicates the picture by triangulating his play against one by Shakespeare and one by Jonson – and by alluding, at specific points, to works by Aristophanes, Thomas Kyd, and Edmund Spenser.

It was the new practice of feminist criticism that broke that critical monopoly, restoring attention to female writers such as Margaret Cavendish, and breaking down the seeming wholeness of all canons by calling attention to their separate treatments of (and effects on) men and women. Although at least one nineteenth-century scholar pronounced Fletcher's female characters 'superior to those of almost any dramatist' – 'not excepting Shakespeare's' – that preference could have only limited impact in a culture and profession that devalued women and overvalued Shakespeare.[87] After all, when John Dryden contrasted Shakespeare's 'more *Masculine*' genius with Fletcher's '*more soft and Womanish*' mind, it was not to praise Fletcher (or Cavendish).[88] The praise of Fletcher's women, voiced in 1812, was immediately contradicted by a much more influential critic, Coleridge, who insisted that 'of all our writers [Shakespeare] alone had truly drawn the female character with that mixture

of the real and the ideal which belongs to woman.'[89] By contrast
with what he calls the 'sweet' and 'holy' women of Shakespeare, 'the
female characters in the plays of Beaumont and Fletcher are, when
of the light kind, not decent; when heroic, complete viragos'.[90]
Coleridge's only annotation on his copy of *The Woman's Prize* was
to cross out Maria's ambition to redeem her 'country' (1.2.67) and
replace it with 'sex': a man might reform an entire country, but even
the most ambitious woman could do nothing beyond the sphere of
her own gender.[91] Not until the 1986 publication of Woodbridge's
Women in the English Renaissance did scholars begin to take Fletcher's
comedy seriously.[92] Even then, response was slow, in part owing to
the unavailability of a modernized edition.

This is not to say the play was completely ignored in the twentieth century. It was translated into Russian in 1938. Old-spelling editions were produced by George Ferguson in 1966 – the first edition
of the play on its own, outside of a larger collection – and by Graham
Adams in 1974. Neither editor, however, seemed to appreciate or
even grasp the play's gender politics (Ferguson views Petruccio as
unaffected by the taming), and indeed both undervalued Fletcher's
artistic achievement. Adams, astonishingly, declares on the first page
of his introduction that the play 'has little literary merit'.[93] (Why edit
it then?) Ferguson praises Fletcher's comic vision and verbal 'color',
but also accuses him of reliance on 'stock characters'[94] – a complaint
that appeared once or twice in reviews of the recent RSC double-
billing. It also shows up in the introduction to *The Woman's Prize* in
the 2002 Norton anthology – the play's first appearance in such a
selection of the best plays of the English Renaissance. Although Eric
Rasmussen celebrates Fletcher's 'brilliant comic irony', he still characterizes the play as a 'sequel' founded on a 'Shakespearean model',
dismisses Moroso as 'a stock figure', and describes the plotting as
'generic'.[95]

The question of the play's literary merit has not quite been
answered by recent criticism, much of which focuses on gender
politics. That emphasis reflects a larger imbalance within the scholarly community: issues of literary achievement were almost entirely
ignored in the very decades when the play returned to prominence.
Until the rise of a new aestheticism, more theoretically sophisticated
than the old formalism, critics will not be well-equipped to tackle
such questions in a way that does not simply repeat the banalities
of Victorian or Modernist bias.[96] More specifically, the literary merit
of *The Tamer Tamed* cannot be determined without serious attention

to the play's language. Adams did not provide a commentary at all, and neither did the 2003 edition of the RSC adaptation (which changed the names of Moroso, Sophocles, Jaques, and Pedro to Gremio, Hortensio, Grumio, and Peter, conflating Fletcher's characters with Shakespeare's). Ferguson's 'Critical Notes' were primarily textual, and, although the Norton commentary is undoubtedly the best yet published, the textbook anthology format necessarily restricted the editors to glosses and paraphrases. Our notes try to encourage a more informed attention to Fletcher's semantic play.

'Character' is created, in part, linguistically. But it is also created through performance. In the RSC double-billing, the interiority of the lead characters in Shakespeare's *Shrew* was entirely interpolated. Doran complicated Petruccio by adding the subtext of the character's grief for his father, having him wear a black armband and visibly mourn by Daddy's portrait. And Katherine the 'shrew' is notoriously difficult for actresses, owing to the paucity of lines given her and the question of whether her transformation is genuine. As viewers and readers of Shakespeare, we bring four centuries of creative theatrical and critical interpretation to the text. Fletcher's play, by contrast, is a blank slate.

As a blank slate, though, it is also brimming with potential. A remarkable number of reviews of the *Taming/Tamer* productions emphasized the actors' evident excitement in staging the two plays: it seems clear that excitement derived largely if not entirely from Fletcher. Indeed, Doran confessed that reading Fletcher's play 'took [his] breath away'.[97] And there is a sense of breathlessness, of the excitement of carnival and of revolution, that runs through the play. The quality of Fletcher's work that Doran calls 'lightness of tone' should not obscure the underlying seriousness of the play's artistic vision. The men's verbal violence is only one aspect of this weight, this seriousness. Gordon McMullan aptly limns out the play's tonal balance:

> There is far more to the play than the earnest promotion of social policy. In its comic depictions of female rebellion, of carnivalesque anarchy and of male bonding premised on the fear of women, *The Tamer Tamed* offers us not only a hilarious drama of inversion but also a rumbustious twist of a tale we thought we knew perfectly well. Above all, it offers us Maria, whose triumph on Petruchio's own turf and subsequent acknowledgment of his love force us to recognise the tenuousness of the social contract by which men and women negotiate their shared world.[98]

In a world where women and men still struggle to understand one another – a world in which domestic violence runs rampant and psychologists write best-sellers with titles like *Women are from Venus, Men are from Mars* – those of us here on earth need Fletcher's play now no less than in 1610.

NOTES

1 Hélène Cixous and Catherine Clément, *The Newly Born Woman*, tr. Betsy Wing (Minneapolis: University of Minnesota Press, 1986), p. 98.

2 Gordon McMullan, *The Politics of Unease in the Plays of John Fletcher* (Amherst: University of Massachusetts Press, 1994), pp. 1–12 (early life), pp. 267–8 (canon and chronology).

3 *'Brief Lives', chiefly of Contemporaries, set down by John Aubrey, between the Years 1669 & 1696*, ed. Andrew Clark (Oxford: Clarendon, 1898), I:96.

4 Jonathan Dollimore, *Sexual Dissidence: Augustine to Wilde, Freud to Foucault* (Oxford: Clarendon, 1991), pp. 300–6.

5 G. E. Bentley, *The Jacobean and Caroline Stage*, 7 vols (Oxford: Clarendon, 1941–68), 4:753.

6 McMullan, *Politics of Unease*, pp. 14–27.

7 Philip J. Finkelpearl, *Court and Country Politics in the Plays of Beaumont and Fletcher* (Princeton: Princeton University Press, 1990), pp. 34–5.

8 Samuel A. Tannenbaum, 'A Hitherto Unpublished John Fletcher Autograph', *Journal of English and Germanic Philology* 28 (1929), 35–40.

9 See William B. Warner, 'The "Woman Writer" and Feminist Literary History; or, how the success of feminist literary history has compromised the conceptual coherence of its lead character, the "woman writer"', *Journal of Early Modern Cultural Studies* 4 (2004), 187–96.

10 Kim F. Hall, 'Beauty and the Beast of Whiteness: Teaching Race and Gender', *Shakespeare Quarterly* 47 (1996), 461–75.

11 N. W. Bawcutt, *The Control and Censorship of Caroline Drama: The Records of Sir Henry Herbert, Master of the Revels 1623–73* (Oxford: Clarendon Press, 1996), pp. 182–3.

12 Richard Dutton, '"Discourse in the players, though no disobedience": Sir Henry Herbert's Problems with the Players and Archbishop Laud, 1632–34', *Ben Jonson Journal* 5 (1998), 37–62.

13 *Tamer* rejects the 'cleanly way of poetry' that Herbert praised in James Shirley's 1633 comedy *The Young Admiral*, a play 'free from oaths, prophaness, or obsceanes' (Bawcutt, ed., *Records*, 180).

14 Bawcutt, ed., *Records*, p. 61.

15 On early modern profanity and its censorship in drama see Celia R. Daileader, *Eroticism on the Renaissance Stage: Transcendance, Desire, and the Limits of the Visible* (Cambridge: Cambridge University Press, 1998), pp. 107–31.

16 3 Jac. I, c. 21: 27 May 1606. For a full discussion of this law and its editorial implications see Gary Taylor, ''Swounds Revisited: Theatrical, Editorial, and Literary Expurgation', in Gary Taylor and John Jowett, *Shakespeare Reshaped 1606–1623* (Oxford: Clarendon, 1993), pp. 51–106.

17 Perkins, *A Golden Chaine* (London, 1600), p. 723.

18 Meg Powers Livingston, 'Herbert's Censorship of Female Power in Fletcher's *The Woman's Prize*', *Medieval and Renaissance Drama in England* 13 (2000), 226.

19 Richard Dutton, '"Discourse in the Players, though No Disobedience": Sir Henry Herbert's Problems with the Players and Archbishop Laud, 1632–34', *Ben Jonson Journal* 5 (1998), 37–62.

20 Molly Easo Smith, 'John Fletcher's Response to the Gender Debate: *The Woman's Prize* and *The Taming of the Shrew*', *Papers in Language and Literature* 31 (1995), 38–60.

21 Fiona McNeill, 'Gynocentric London Spaces: (Re)Locating Masterless Women in Early Stuart Drama', *Renaissance Drama* 28 (1997), 215–17.

22 McNeill, 'Gynocentric London Spaces', p. 217; Smith, 'John Fletcher's Response', p. 42.

23 For an account of Huntington's involvement in the Midland riots see McMullan, *Politics of Unease*, pp. 37–55.

24 Baldwin Maxwell, 'The Woman's Prize, or The Tamer Tamed', *Modern Philology* 32 (1935), 353–64; Gary Taylor, 'The Date and Original Venue of Fletcher's *Tamer Tamed*' (forthcoming).

25 For a survey of scholarship on the dearth of 1607–9 see Gary Taylor, 'Gender, Hunger, Horror: The History and Significance of *The Bloody Banquet*', *Journal of Early Modern Cultural Studies* 1 (2001), 9–10.

26 James F. Larkin and Paul L. Hughes, ed., *Stuart Royal Proclamations*. Volume I: *Royal Proclamations of King James I 1603–1625* (Oxford: Clarendon, 1973), pp. 200–2.

27 *Calendar of State Papers and Manuscripts relating to English Affairs, existing in the archives and collections of Venice*, vol. XI, *1607–1610*, ed. Horatio F. Brown (London: Her Majesty's Stationery Office, 1904), pp. 212–13.

28 Andrew McRae, *Literature, Satire, and the Early Stuart State* (Cambridge: Cambridge University Press, 2004), pp. 46–9, 69–75.

29 Finkelpearl, *Court and Country Politics*, pp. 20–5 (Beaumont on Lady Markham, Jonson on Cecilia Bulstrode).

30 Adam Fox, *Oral and Literate Culture in England 1500–1700* (Oxford: Oxford University Press, 2000).

31 For the plague see Leeds Barroll, *Politics, Plague, and Shakespeare's Theater: The Stuart Years* (Ithaca: Cornell University Press, 1991), pp. 173–84.

32 Susan Amussen, *An Ordered Society: Gender and Class in Early Modern England* (New York: Columbia University Press, 1988), pp. 42–7.

33 Mark Brietenberg, *Anxious Masculinity in Early Modern England* (Cambridge: Cambridge University Press, 1996), pp. 21–6, 193–7.

34 Elizabeth A. Foyster, *Manhood in Early Modern England: Honour, Sex and Marriage* (London: Longman, 1999), pp. 191–2.

35 Martin Ingram, 'Ridings, Rough Music and the "reform of popular culture" in Early Modern England', *Past and Present* 105 (1984), 79–113.

36 David Underdown, 'The Taming of the Scold: The Enforcement of Patriarchal Authority in Early Modern England', in Anthony Fletcher and John Stevenson, ed., *Order and Disorder in Early Modern England*, (Cambridge: Cambridge University Press, 1985), pp. 116–36.

37 On Fletcher's knowledge of Jonson's play see Charles Mill Gayley, *Representative English Comedies*, 4 vols (New York: Macmillan, 1914–36), 3:lxvi; Taylor, 'Date and Venue'.

38 On the dating of *Shrew* see Gary Taylor, 'The Canon and Chronology of Shakespeare's Plays', in Stanley Wells, Gary Taylor, *et al.*, *William Shakespeare: A Textual Companion* (Oxford: Clarendon, 1987), pp. 109–11.

39 Coppélia Kahn influentially argued that Katherine's final speech 'completes the fantasy of male dominance, but also mocks it as mere fantasy' (*Man's Estate: Masculine Identity in Shakespeare* (Berkeley: University of California Press, 1981), p. 116). This revisionism characterizes the obedience speech 'more as a performance than an expression of sincere belief' (Marianne L. Novy, *Love's Argument: Gender Relations in Shakespeare* (Chapel Hill: University of North Carolina Press, 1984), p. 58). Holly A. Crocker goes so far as to read Fletcher's response to the play as a positive comment on *Shrew*'s gender politics, because Fletcher reads Katherine's taming as inauthentic. Crocker writes that *Tamer Tamed* '*enjoys* the multiplicity implied by Katherine's performance, inviting its audience to take pleasure in the potentialities that her passivity opens up' ('Affective Resistance: Performing Passivity and Playing-a-Part in *The Taming of the Shrew*', *Shakespeare Quarterly* 54 (2003), 142–59 (italics in original)). But this reading fails to take account of what Fletcher's heroine herself says of Katherine: 'She was a fool / And took a scurvy course. Let her be named / 'Mongst those that wish for things but dare not do 'em' (1.2.142–4).

40 Quotations from Shakespeare cite *The Complete Works*, gen. ed. Stanley Wells and Gary Taylor (Oxford: Oxford University Press, 1986).

41 Louis E. Lord, *Aristophanes: His Plays and His Influence* (New York: Cooper Square, 1963), p. 163. Lord notes the subsidiary influence of the *Ecclesiazusae*, which is ignored by other critics, and concludes that 'the English play [*The Tamer Tamed*] is not so coarse as the Greek and there is more interest in the study of female character'.

42 Langbaine, *An Account of the English Dramatic Poets* (London, 1691), p. 217; this paragraph was repeated in John Denham's 'Preface' to *The Works of Mr. Francis Beaumont, and Mr. John Fletcher*, 7 vols (London: Jacob Tonson, 1711), 1:xli.

43 'Introduction', in *The Works of Beaumont & Fletcher*, ed. Dyce, 11 vols (London: Moxon, 1843–46), I:lxiv.

44 Woodbridge, *Women in the English Renaissance: Literature and the Nature of Womankind, 1540–1620* (Urbana: University of Illinois Press, 1984), pp. 244–71.

45 Bawcutt, ed., *Records*, p. 185.

46 Frances E. Dolan, ed., *The Taming of the Shrew: Texts and Contexts* (Boston: Bedford, 1996), pp. 254–7.

47 On the play's pervasive equestrian imagery see Lynda E. Boose, 'Scolding Brides and Bridling Scolds: Taming a Woman's Unruly Member', *Shakespeare Quarterly* 42 (1991), 179–213, and Joan Hartwig, 'Horses and Women in *The Taming of the Shrew*', *Huntington Library Quarterly* 45 (1982), 285–94.

48 See Natalie Zemon Davis's chapter on 'The Woman on Top', in *Society and Culture in Early Modern France* (Stanford: Stanford University Press, 1975), pp. 124–51.

49 For 'leaky' women see Gail Kern Paster, *The Body Embarrassed: Drama and the Disciplines of Shame in Early Modern England* (Ithaca: Cornell University Press, 1993).

50 Mikhail Bakhtin, *Rabelais and His World*, trans. Helen Iswolsky (Bloomington: Indiana University Press, 1984). For an influential development and critique of Bakhtin's theory of the carnivalesque see Peter Stallybrass and Allon White, *The Politics and Poetics of Transgression* (London: Methuen, 1986).

51 For the event and its reflection in the drama of the period see Sara Jayne Steen, 'The Crime of Marriage: Arbella Stuart and *The Duchess of Malfi*', *Sixteenth Century Journal* 22 (1991), 61–76.

52 Kathleen McLuskie notes the intensifying language of male violence in these sequences; her reading connects the play to women's entry into the free market, and the threat to male power this represented (*Renaissance Dramatists* (Atlantic Highlands, NJ: Humanities International Press, 1989), pp. 214–18).

53 Emily Detmer, 'Civilizing Subordination: Domestic Violence and *The Taming of the Shrew*', *Shakespeare Quarterly* 48 (1997), 273–94.

54 See Parker's insightful discussion of the notion of literary *copia* in *Literary Fat Ladies: Rhetoric, Gender, Property* (London: Methuen, 1987), pp. 8–35.

55 Caroline Walker Bynum, *Holy Feast and Holy Fast: The Religious Significance of Food to Medieval Women* (Berkeley: University of California Press, 1987); Susan Bordo, *Unbearable Weight: Feminism, Western Culture, and the Body* (Berkeley: University of California Press, 1993).

56 Margaret Cavendish, *The Convent of Pleasure and Other Plays*, ed. Anne Shaver (Baltimore: Johns Hopkins University Press); *CCXI Sociable Letters written by the Lady Marchioness of Newcastle* (1664), Letter CXXIII.

57 Taylor, 'Date and Original Venue'.

58 For a summary of what we know about the Whitefriars and its companies see William Ingram, 'The Playhouse as an Investment, 1607–1614: Thomas Woodford and Whitefriars', *Medieval and Renaissance Drama in England* 2 (1985), 209–30.

59 Emrys Jones, 'The First West-End Comedy' (1982), in E. A. J. Hongimann, ed., *British Academy Shakespeare Lectures 1980–89* (Oxford: Oxford University Press, 1993), pp. 85–116.

60 Gary Taylor, 'The Structure of Performance: Act-Intervals in the London Theatres, 1576–1642', in Gary Taylor and John Jowett, *Shakespeare Reshaped, 1606–1623* (Oxford: Clarendon Press, 1993), pp. 3–50.

61 For a reading of the play that emphasizes how Maria sets out 'to seize control of space', see Daileader, *Eroticism on the Renaissance Stage*, pp. 53–65.

62 Will Fisher, 'Staging the Beard: Masculinity in Early Modern English Culture', in Jonathan Gil Harris and Natasha Korda, eds, *Staged Properties in Early Modern English Drama* (Cambridge: Cambrdige University Press, 2002), pp. 230–57.

63 Gary Taylor, 'Shakespeare Plays on Renaissance Stages', in Sarah Stanton and Stanley Wells, ed., *The Cambridge Companion to Shakespeare*

in the Theatre (Cambridge: Cambridge University Press, 2001), pp. 18–19.

64 Ford's elegy, extant only in manuscript, was first printed in Brian Vickers, ed., *English Renaissance Literary Criticism* (Oxford: Clarendon Press, 1999), pp. 541–5.

65 The Prologue, printed after the play in 1647, has been included in editions of the play ever since, but it refers to Fletcher in the third person and the past tense, so it must have been written after his death; stylistically, too, it cannot be Fletcher's work.

66 Thomas Jordan, 'A Prologue to the Comedy call'd The Tamer tamed', from *A Nursery of Novelties in Variety of Poetry* (London, 1665), pp. 20–1.

67 *The Diary of Samuel Pepys*, ed. R. C. Latham and W. Matthews, 11 vols (London: Bell & Hyman, 1971), 1:278, 2:145.

68 William Van Lennep, ed., *The London Stage, Part I: 1660–1700* (Carbondale: Southern Illinois University Press, 1965), pp. 8, 11, 12, 35, 45, 48, 225.

69 A. C. Sprague, *Beaumont and Fletcher on the Restoration Stage* (Cambridge: Harvard University Press, 1926), p. 46.

70 Richard Owen Cambridge, 'Epilogue Spoken at Drury-Lane Theatre, By Miss Pritchard, in the Character of Maria in the Tamer tamed: 1760', *Works*, p. 319.

71 In the subsequent decades there is evidence for three rather obscure additional productions, one at Queensland University in Australia, one in New York, and one in Seattle, but we have found little information about these revivals.

72 Thomas Larque, *Shakespeare Bulletin* 21 (2003), 76–82.

73 See Kahn, *Man's Estate*, pp. 115–16; Dolan, *Taming*, pp. 24–9; Carol Rutter, *Clamorous Voices: Shakespeare's Women Today* (London: Women's Press, 1988), pp. 1–25.

74 Michael Billington, *Guardian*, 11 April 2003, 'The Taming of the Shrew/The Tamer Tamed', p. 30.

75 Kate Basset, *Independent on Sunday*, 13 April 2003, p. 9.

76 Charles Spencer, *The Daily Telegraph*, 11 April 2003, p. 20.

77 Susannah Clapp, 'The Shrew Must Go on – and on', *The Observer*, 13 April 2003, p. 11.

78 Aleks Sierz, *Times Educational Supplement*, 4 April 2003.

79 Thomas Seward, 'Preface', in *The Works of Mr. F. Beaumont and Mr. J. Fletcher*, ed. Lewis Theobald, Thomas Seward, and Mr Sympson of Gainsborough (London: J. R. Tonson: 1750), 1:liii, lvi.

80 Leigh Hunt, ed., *Beaumont and Fletcher; or, the finest scenes and other beauties of those two poets, now first selected from the whole of their works, to the exclusion of whatever is morally objectionable* . . . (London, 1855), pp. x–xi, xv.

81 J. S. Fletcher, ed., *The Plays of Beaumont and Fletcher* (London and Newcastle: Walter Scott, 1887), pp. xxii, xvii.

82 *The Dramatick Works of Beaumont and Fletcher*, ed. George Coleman the elder, 10 vols (London, 1778), vol. 8, p. 375.

83 Henry Weber, ed., *The Works of Beaumont and Fletcher*, 14 vols (Edinburgh: Ballantyne, 1812), 5:394–95; Alexander Dyce, ed., *The Works of Beaumont & Fletcher*, 11 vols (London: Moxon, 1843–46), 7:206.

84 On the Romantic and Victorian climax of Shakespeare's reputation see Gary Taylor, *Reinventing Shakespeare: A Cultural History from the Restoration to the Present* (New York: Grove Weidenfeld, 1989) and 'Afterword: The Incredible Shrinking Bard', in Christy Desmet and Robert Sawyer, ed., *Shakespeare and Appropriation* (New York: Routledge, 1999), pp. 197–205.

85 Seward, 'Preface', in *Works* (1750), I:xv.

86 For the logic of bardolatry see Gary Taylor, 'Power, Pathos, Character', in Christy Desmet and Robert Sawyer, ed., *Harold Bloom and the Interpretation of Shakespeare* (New York: Palgrave, 2001), pp. 43–64.

87 Weber, *Beaumont and Fletcher*, 1:lxxiv, lxxxi.

88 'The Grounds of Criticism in Tragedy', in *The Works of John Dryden*, ed. Vinton Dearing *et al.*, XIII (1984): 233, 247.

89 Roberta Florence Brinkley, ed., *Coleridge on the Seventeenth Century* (New York: Greenwood, 1968), pp. 649–52; Samuel Taylor Coleridge, *Lectures 1808–1819 On Literature*, ed. R. A. Foakes, 2 vols (Princeton: Princeton University Press, 1987), 1:297–8.

90 Coleridge, *Lectures*, 2:269.

91 *The Collected Works of Samuel Taylor Coleridge*, vol. 12, *Marginalia*, part I, ed. George Whalley (Princeton: Princeton University Press, 1980), p. 401.

92 Woodbridge, *Women*, pp. 197–8, 240, 250, 282, 326.

93 Graham Cleavern Adams, ed., 'John Fletcher's *The Woman's Prize*': A Thesis Submitted in Partial Fulfillment of the Requirements for the Degree of Doctor of Philosophy (University of New Brunswick, 1974), p. viii.

94 John Fletcher, *The Woman's Prize, or, The Tamer Tamed: A Critical Edition*, ed. George B. Ferguson (The Hague: Mouton & Co., 1966), pp. 14–15.

95 Eric Rasmussen, 'The Woman's Prize', in *English Renaissance Drama: A Norton Anthology*, gen. ed. David Bevington (New York: W. W. Norton, 2002), pp. 1215–18.

96 For harbingers of an emergent new aestheticism see the essays collected in Mark David Rasmussen, ed., *Renaissance Literature and Its Formal Engagements* (New York: Palgrave, 2002) and Frank B. Farrell, *Why Does Literature Matter* (Ithaca: Cornell University Press, 2004).

97 Gregory Doran, 'The Antidote to Shakespeare', *Guardian Review* (2 April 2003).

98 Gordon McMullen, 'Introduction', in John Fletcher, *The Tamer Tamed* (RSC London: Nick Hern Books, 2003), p. xvii.

THE TAMER TAMED;
OR, THE WOMAN'S
PRIZE

Tamer Tamed] alluding to Shakespeare's *The Taming of the Shrew.*

Woman's Prize] a paradox: prizes were won in military, athletic, chivalric, and educational contests, from all of which women were systematically excluded. There was no social institution in which women could win a prize. For a posthumous prologue see Introduction pp. 26–7.

THE PERSONS REPRESENTED IN THE PLAY

[*Men:*]

PETRUCCIO, *an Italian gentleman,* [*widowed, and newly remarried;*] *husband to Maria.*

SOPHOCLES: }
TRANIO: } *two gentlemen, friends to Petruccio.*

MOROSO, *an old rich doting citizen, suitor to Livia.*

ROLAND, *a young gentleman, in love with Livia.*

PETRONIUS, *father to Maria and Livia.*

JAQUES: }
PEDRO: } *two witty servants to Petruccio.*

WATCHMEN

[SERVANT to Petronius]

Porters

[Servants]

Women:

MARIA, *a chaste witty lady*: } *the two daughters*
LIVIA, [*a lady, in love with*] Roland: } *of Petronius.*

BIANCA, [*a lady,*] *their cousin.*

CITY [WIFE], *drunk*: }
COUNTRY [WIFE], *drunk*: } *to the relief of the ladies.*
[THREE COUNTRY WENCHES]: }

THE SCENE: *London.*

Act 1

Enter MOROSO, SOPHOCLES, *and* TRANIO *with rosemary as from a wedding.*

Moroso. God give 'em joy!
Tranio.   Amen.
Sophocles.   Amen, say I too.
     The pudding's now i'th' proof. Alas, poor wench,
     Through what a mine of patience must thou work
     Ere thou know'st good hour more!
Tranio.   'Tis too true, certain,
     Methinks her father has dealt harshly with her,   5
     Exceeding harshly, and not like a father,
     To match her to this dragon. I protest
     I pity the poor gentlewoman.
Moroso.   Methinks now
     He's not so terrible as people think him.
Sophocles. [*Aside to Tranio*] This old thief flatters out of mere
     devotion   10

1.1] Between the church and Petronius's house.

1.1.0.1. rosemary] a fragrant evergreen herb, used at weddings and funerals as an emblem of memory and immortality.

1. *God*] (Here and occasionally elsewhere the manuscript has been censored, substituting 'heaven' for 'God'.)

2. *The pudding's . . . proof*] (Alluding to the proverb 'The proof of the pudding is in the eating').

wench] (An affectionate, patronizing slang term for a young woman, comparable to the modern 'girl'; referring to Maria.)

3. *mine*] large amount; store.

4. *good hour more*] i.e., another happy moment.

certain] certainly (modifying the preceding and following clauses).

7. *this dragon*] i.e., Petruccio (comparing Maria to Andromeda, whose father sacrificed her to a sea-dragon).

protest] declare.

10. *thief*] unscrupulous greedy person.

45

To please the father for his second daughter.
Tranio. [*Aside to Sophocles*] But shall he have her?
Sophocles. [*Aside to Tranio*]   Yes, when I have Rome.
And yet the father's for him.
Moroso.   I'll assure ye,
I hold him a good man.
Sophocles.   Yes, sure, a wealthy –
But whether a good woman's man is doubtful.   15
Tranio. Would 'twere no worse!
Moroso.   What though his other wife,
Out of her most abundant stubbornness,
Out of her daily hue and cries upon him –
For, sure, she was a rebel – turned his temper
And forced him blow as high as she? Does't follow   20
He must retain that long-since-buried tempest
To this soft maid?
Sophocles.   I fear it.
Tranio.   So do I too,
And so far that, if God had made me woman
And his wife that must be –
Moroso.   What would you do, sir?
Tranio. I would learn to eat coals with an angry cat   25
And spit fire at him. I would, to prevent him,
Do all the ramping roaring tricks a whore,
Being drunk and tumbling-ripe, would tremble at.
There is no safety else, nor moral wisdom,
To be a wife, and his.
Sophocles.   So I should think, too.   30

---

11. *for*] in order to win.

12. *when . . . Rome*] i.e., never.

14. *hold*] consider.

16. *his other wife*] Katherine, depicted in Shakespeare's *The Taming of the Shrew*.

19. *turned his temper*] altered his calm temperament.

20. *blow . . . she*] storm as blusteringly as she, Katherine.

21. *long-since-buried*] (Petruccio is a widower.)

25. *eat . . . cat*] (Hot coals in a wet mouth would produce a hissing sound; anger is often associated with heat, and women with cats.)

26. *prevent*] anticipate.

27. *ramping*] raging, behaving like a wild animal rearing up on its hind legs.

28. *tumbling-ripe*] ready to (1) fall prostrate; (2) have sex.

29. *else*] otherwise.

Tranio. For yet the bare remembrance of his first wife –
    I tell ye on my knowledge, and a truth too –
    Will make him start in's sleep, and very often
    Cry out for cudgels, cowl-staves, anything,
    Hiding his breeches, out of fear her ghost   35
    Should walk and wear 'em yet. Since his first marriage
    He is no more the still Petruccio
    Than I am Babylon.
Sophocles.   He's a good fellow,
    And, by my troth, I love him; but to think
    A fit match for this tender soul –   40
Tranio. Her very sound, if she but say her prayers
    Louder than men talk treason, makes him tinder.
    The motion of a dial, when he's testy,
    Is the same trouble to him as a waterwork.
    She must do nothing of herself, not eat,   45
    Sleep, say 'Sir, how do ye?', make her ready, piss,
    Unless he bid her.
Sophocles.   He will bury her,
    Ten pounds to twenty shillings, within this three weeks.

---

31. *bare*] mere.

33. *in's*] in his.

34. *cudgels*] (Often associated with Petruccio's wife-taming, like the riding-whip of later stagings of *Shrew.*)

cowl-staves] stout poles used to carry a heavy burden, supported on the shoulders of two bearers. Hence, (1) a common household implement and civilian weapon; (2) a pole used to carry someone derisively through the streets – a popular punishment inflicted on husbands dominated by their wives.

37. *still*] (1) same; (2) quiet, mild.

38. *Babylon*] i.e., a violent outlaw. In an old ballad, 'Babylon' kills two sisters before the third identifies him as their long-lost brother, 'baby Lon'.

42. *tinder*] (1) flammable material, used to kindle fires or ignite gunpowder; (2) punningly opposite to 'tender' and easily lit by a 'match' (line 40).

43. *dial*] hand of a clock.

44. *waterwork*] (noisy) machinery for re-directing river water.

45. *of*] by.

46. *make her ready*] get dressed.

48. *twenty shillings*] one pound sterling (i.e., ten to one) (equivalent to the cost of forty-four loaves of bread at the time).

Tranio. I'll be your half.
Moroso.   He loves her most extremely,
    And so long 'twill be honeymoon.

                    Enter JAQUES *with a pot of wine.*

                                        Now, Jaques!   50
        You are a busy man, I am sure.
Jaques.   Yes, certain,
    This old sport must have eggs –
Sophocles.   Not yet this ten days.
Jaques. Sweet gentlemen, with muscatel.
Tranio.   That's right, sir.
Moroso. This fellow broods his master. – Speed you, Jaques.
Sophocles. We shall be for you presently.
Jaques.   Your Worships   55
    Shall have it rich and neat and, o' my conscience,
    As welcome as Our Lady Day. Oh, my old sir,
    When shall we see Your Worship run at ring?
    That hour, a standing were worth money.
Moroso.   So, sir.

-----

49. *I'll be your half*] I will put up half the amount you have wagered, in exchange for getting half the winnings. The same phrase occurs at *Shrew* 5.2.84. Fletcher's play begins, as Shakespeare's ends, with a wager on Petruccio's relationship with his new wife.

50. *so long*] i.e., three weeks.

52. *old*] ancient, primitive (but perhaps also alluding to Petruccio's age).
sport] (Often used of sexual activity.)
eggs] (Considered an aphrodisiac.)

53. *muscatel*] a sweet wine. (Wine in general was believed to enhance sexual potency.)

54. *This ... master*] This servant is solicitous for his master, Petruccio, and hovers protectively over him like a brooding hen.
Speed you] May you have good success.

55. *be for you*] have need of you.
Your Worships] Your Honours, good sirs.

56. *it*] i.e., the wine I will bring you.
neat] straight, not diluted with water.

57. *Our Lady Day*] feast celebrating the Virgin Mary, 25 March, the Feast of the Annunciation (coincident with the beginning of spring).

58. *run at ring*] (1) engage in the chivalric sport in which a tilter, riding on horseback at full speed, tries to thrust the point of the lance through a ring; (2) try to penetrate a woman.

59. *standing*] (1) standing place or room for spectators at the tiltyard (2) erection.

Jaques. Upon my little honesty, your mistress,   60
 If I have any speculation,
 Must think this single thrumming of a fiddle,
 Without a bow, but even poor sport.
Moroso.   You're merry.
Jaques. Would I were wise too. So, God bless Your Worships.
              Exit.

Tranio. [*To Moroso*] The fellow tells you true.
Sophocles. [*To Moroso*]   When is the day, man?   65
 Come, come, you'd steal a marriage.
Moroso.   Nay, believe me.
 But when her father pleases, I am ready,
 And all my friends shall know it.
Tranio.   Why not now?
 One charge had served for both.
Moroso.   There's reason in't.
Sophocles. Called Roland.
Moroso.   Will ye walk? They'll think we are lost.   70
 Come, gentlemen.   [*Exit.*]
Tranio. [*To Sophocles*] You have whipped him now.
Sophocles. So will he never the wench, I hope.
Tranio.   I wish it.   *Exeunt.*

---

60. *your mistress*] the woman to whom you devote your attentions as a wooer, Livia.

61. *speculation*] powers of intelligent observation.

62–3. *single . . . bow*] another impotence joke. 'Fiddling' was a euphemism for sexual intercourse: the bow represents the erect penis, the fiddle and its strings the female genitals. Jaques implies that Moroso's bride, lacking a capable 'bow', would have to be content with unmarried ('single') digital stimulation (thrumming).

66. *steal a marriage*] elope.

69. *One . . . both*] It would have been thriftier if you had combined two weddings in one (as a wedding and funeral are huddled together in *Hamlet*).
in't] in it.

70. *Called Roland*] i.e., The reason for the delay is that you have a rival, Roland, for the hand of Livia.
They'll] The rest of the wedding party will.

71. *whipped*] beaten.

72. *So . . . wench*] The 'whipping' Sophocles would prevent here is most likely sexual, playing on the horse-and-rider metaphors which pervade the text (a horse is urged forward by whipping). None the less, the literal sense of whipping the bride is not irrelevant, as it highlights the latent violence and subjugation intrinsic in the notion of wife-taming.

I.2

Enter ROLAND *and* LIVIA.

Roland. Nay, Livia, if you'll go away tonight,
 If your affections be not made of words –
Livia. I love you, and you know how dearly, Roland. –
 Is there none near us? – My affections ever
 Have been your servants. With what superstition   5
 I have ever sainted you –
Roland.   Why then, take this way.
Livia. 'Twill be a childish and less prosperous course
 Than his that knows not care. Why should we do
 Our honest and our hearty loves such wrong
 To over-run our fortunes?
Roland.   Then you flatter.   10
Livia. Alas, you know I cannot.
Roland.   What hope's left else,
 But flying, to enjoy ye?
Livia.   None so far.
 For let it be admitted, we have time
 And all things now in other expectation,
 My father's bent against us. What but ruin   15
 Can such a by-way bring us? If your fears
 Would let you look with my eyes, I would show you,
 And certain, how our staying here would win us
 A course, though somewhat longer, yet far surer.

I.2] Petronius's house. Wedding feasts – which could last several days, and include consummation of the marriage – were often held at the home of the bride's father. This places Maria between the lapsed authority of her father and the not-yet-enforced authority of her huband.

4. *Is . . . us?*] Can no one overhear us?

6. *take this way*] follow the course I've proposed (elopement).

8. *his . . . care*] the course of someone completely careless.

10. *over-run*] run beyond.

flatter] deceive.

12. *flying*] fleeing, escaping.

13–15. *For . . . us*] Although we have an opportunity and everyone is distracted by other business (Petruccio's wedding), nevertheless my father's opposition remains as an obstacle.

16. *by-way*] indirect course.

Roland. And then Moroso has ye.
Livia.   No such matter.   20
    For hold this certain: begging, stealing, whoring,
    Selling (which is a sin unpardonable)
    Of counterfeit cods, or musty English cracus,
    Switches, or stones for th' toothache, sooner finds me
    Than that drawn fox Moroso.
Roland.   But his money!   25
    If wealth may win you –
Livia.   If a hog may be
    High priest among the Jews! His money, Roland?
    O Love forgive me! What a faith hast thou?
    Why, can his money kiss me?
Roland.   Yes.
Livia.   Behind,
    Laid out upon a petticoat. Or grasp me,   30
    While I cry, 'Oh, good thank you'? (O' my troth,
    Thou mak'st me merry with thy fear.) – Or lie with me
    As you may do? Alas, what fools you men are!
    His mouldy money? Half a dozen riders
    That cannot sit but stamped fast to their saddles?   35
    No, Roland, no man shall make use of me.
    My beauty was born free, and free I'll give it

22–4. *Selling . . . toothache*] (As a member of the gentry class, Livia regards the retail trade in trivial accessories as the ultimate degradation, worse than being a courtesan.)

23. *counterfeit cods*] (1) small bags resembling testicles, containing spurious or adulterated civet or musk (perfume) (2) codpieces.

cracus] brand of tobacco sold in London c. 1610–16.

24. *Switches*] riding whips.

stones] testicles of an animal (used for medicinal purposes).

25. *drawn*] disemboweled; stuffed.

26–7. *If . . . Jews!*] An impossible condition; orthodox Jews are forbidden to eat pork.

29. *Behind*] On the posterior.

30. *Laid out*] (1) spent; (2) placed.

32. *lie*] have sex.

34. *riders*] gold coins upon which the figure of a horseman is stamped.

35. *cannot sit*] (Livia continues the equestrian innuendo: unlike a lover, the coins cannot sit on her or ride her sexually.)

36. *make use of me*] (1) use me as a sexual object; (2) make a profit from me, as usury accumulates interest on loaned money.

To him that loves, not buys me. You yet doubt me?
Roland. I cannot say I doubt ye.
Livia.   Go thy ways!
    Thou art the prettiest puling piece of passion.   40
    I' faith, I will not fail thee.
Roland.   I had rather –
Livia. Prithee, believe me. If I do not carry it
    For both our goods –
Roland.   But –
Livia.   What 'but'?
Roland.   I would tell you.
Livia. I know all you can tell me. All's but this:
    You would have me, and lie with me. Is't not so?   45
Roland. Yes.
Livia.   Why, you shall. Will that content you? Go.
Roland. I am very loath to go.

                Enter BIANCA *and* MARIA.

Livia.   Now, o' my conscience,
    Thou art an honest fellow. Here's my sister.
    Go, prithee, go. This kiss, and credit me: [*They kiss.*]
    Ere I am three nights older I am for thee.   50
    You shall hear what I do.
Roland.   I had rather feel it.
Livia. Farewell.
Roland.   Farewell.   *Exit Roland.*
Livia. [*Aside*]   Alas, poor fool, how it looks!
    It would e'en hang itself, should I but cross it.
    For pure love to the matter, I must hatch it.
                [*Livia stands apart.*]
Bianca. Nay, never look for merry hour, Maria,   55
    If now ye make it not. Let not your blushes,

---

    39. *Go thy ways*] Get on with you.
    40. *puling*] whining.
    42. *carry it*] bring it off.
    49. *credit*] believe.
    52. *it*] him (a diminutive, often used of children).
    53. *cross*] contradict.
    54. *matter*] (1) business; (2) female genitals.
    hatch it] devise and develop a plan.

Your modesty and tenderness of spirit
Make you continual anvil to his anger.
Believe me, since his first wife set him going,
Nothing can bind his rage. Take your own counsel;		60
You shall not say that I persuaded you.
Maria. Stay. Shall I do it?
Bianca. Have you a stomach to't?
Maria. I never showed it.
Bianca. 'Twill show the rarer and the stranger in you.		65
But do not say I urged you.
Maria.					I'll do it.
Like Curtius, to redeem my country have I
Leaped into this gulf of marriage.
Farewell, all poorer thoughts but spite and anger,
Till I have wrought a miracle upon him!			70
Bianca. This is brave now,
If you continue it. But your own will lead you.
Maria. Adieu, all tenderness! I dare continue.
Maids that are made of fears and modest blushes,
View me, and love example!				75
I am no more the gentle, tame Maria.
Mistake me not. I have a new soul in me,
Made of a north wind, nothing but a tempest –
And, like a tempest, shall it make all ruins

60–1. *Take . . . you*] Make up your mind to do the right thing; it should be your decision (even if I am urging it).

62. *Stay*] (Bianca moves as though to leave.)

63. *a stomach to't*] the strength or appetite for it.

65. *stranger*] more extraordinary.

67. *Curtius*] Marcus Curtius (362 BCE), Roman hero described by the historian Livy (VII:6). When a gap suddenly appeared in the Forum at Rome, an oracle claimed that it could be closed only by the most precious thing Rome possessed. Cartius saved Rome by sacrificing himself, leaping – fully armed – into the gap, which then closed.

71. *brave*] (1) courageous; (2) excellent.

72. *your . . . you*] remember that this is your decision.

74. *Maids*] (1) unmarried women; (2) virgins; (3) female servants.

75. *love example*] do not simply 'take example' (the usual idiom), but fall in love with an exemplary precedent.

76. *tame*] (Fletcher's play begins with a woman already tame, thus reversing the narrative of *The Taming of the Shrew*.)

          Till I have run my will out.

Bianca.   Here is your sister.   80

Maria. Here is the brave old man's love.

Bianca.   That loves the young man.

Maria. Ay, and hold thee there, wench. What a grief of
          heart is't,
     When Paphos' revels should up-rouse old Night,
     To sweat against a cork, to lie and tell
     The clock o'th' lungs, to rise sport-starved!

Livia.   Dear sister,   85
     Where have you been, you talk thus?

Maria.   Why, at church, wench,
     Where I am tied to talk thus. I am a wife now.

Livia. It seems so, and a modest.

Maria.   You're an ass.
     When thou art married once, thy modesty
     Will never buy three pins.

Livia.   Bless me!

Maria.   From what?   90

Bianca. From such a tame fool as our cousin Livia.

Livia. You are not mad?

Maria.   Yes, wench, and so must you be,
     Or none of our acquaintance – mark me, Livia –

---

     80. *run . . . out*] had my way.

     81. *brave*] (1) courageous; (2) gorgeously dressed (ironic, whether applied
to Moroso or Livia).

     83. *Paphos'*] Paphos was a city in Cyprus sacred to Aphrodite, goddess
of love.

     old Night] (1) primeval darkness; (2) aged Moroso.

     84. *sweat against*] (1) work hard on; (2) waste bodily fluids on.

     cork] (1) cylindrical shape made of dry cork, used as a stopper for a bottle
(2) dry penis.

     84–5. *tell . . . lungs*] count the hours by his snoring or coughing.

     sport-starved] starved of sex.

     87. *tied*] (1) obligated; (2) bound in marriage.

     88. *modest*] (Said ironically.)

     89–90. *When . . . pins*] Once you are married, your modesty is worth
nothing. (Modesty was one of the attributes that made women marriageable;
once married, a woman could no longer use this as a bargaining chip.)

     92. *mad*] (Livia means 'crazy', but Maria takes the word in the sense
'angry'.)

Or indeed fit for our sex. 'Tis bedtime.
Pardon me, yellow Hymen, that I mean   95
Thy offerings to protract, and to keep fasting
My valiant bridegroom.
Livia. [*To Bianca*]   Whither will this woman?
Bianca. You may perceive her end.
Livia.   Or rather, fear it.
Maria. Dare you be partner in't?
Livia.   Leave it, Maria.
I fear I have marked too much. For goodness, leave it.   100
Divest you with obedient hands: to bed.
Maria. To bed? No, Livia. There are comets hang
Prodigious over that yet. There's a fellow
Must yet, before I know that heat – ne'er start, wench –
Be made a man, for yet he is a monster.   105
Here must his head be, Livia.
Livia.   Never hope it.
'Tis as easy with a sieve to scoop the ocean, as
To tame Petruccio.
Maria.   Stay. – Lucina, hear me!
Never unlock the treasure of my womb,
For human fruit to make it capable,   110
Nor never with thy secret hand make brief

---

95. *Hymen*] Roman diety of marriage, traditionally yellow-haired and dressed in yellow.

98. *end*] intent.

100. *marked*] heard.

101. *Divest you*] (1) undress yourself; (2) strip yourself of your possessions and legal rights.

102–3. *There . . . yet*] (Comets were regarded as bad omens.)

103. *fellow*] (Disrespectful slang, implying Maria's equality with Petruccio.)

104. *heat*] sexual pleasure.

ne'er start] don't be startled.

106. *Here*] (There are a number of options for this gesture in performance. Maria might indicate that she will be Petruccio's head, thus reversing the Pauline notion that the husband is the 'head' of the married couple, the wife the 'body'. Or she might indicate a body-part of hers that will be level with his soon-to-be lowered head: her feet, or perhaps, more bawdily, her waist, suggesting cunnilingus.)

108. *tame*] (Again alluding to the title of Shakespeare's play.)

Stay] (Livia is about to leave.)

Lucina] Roman goddess of childbirth.

A mother's labour to me, if I do
Give way unto my married husband's will,
Or be a wife in anything but hopes,
Till I have made him easy as a child   115
And tame as fear! He shall not win a smile
Or a pleased look from this austerity,
Though it would pull another jointure from him
And make him every day another man;
And when I kiss him, till I have my will,   120
May I be barren of delights, and know
Only what pleasure is in dreams and guesses.
Livia. A strange exordium!
Bianca. [*To Maria*]   All the several wrongs
Done by imperious husbands to their wives
These thousand years and upwards, strengthen thee!   125
Thou hast a brave cause.
Maria.   And I'll do it bravely,
Or may I knit my life out ever after.
Livia. In what part of the world got she this spirit? –
Yet pray, Maria, look before you truly:
Besides the disobedience of a wife,   130
Which you will find a heavy imputation
(Which yet I cannot think your own, it shows
So distant from your sweetness) –
Maria.   'Tis, I swear.

---

112. *labour*] birth pangs.

113. *will*] (1) volition; (2) sexual appetite.

115. *easy*] compliant.

117. *this austerity*] (Maria refers to her own stern demeanour.)

118. *jointure*] estate held jointly by a married couple which would be passed to the wife in the event of widowhood.

119. *another*] a new.

123. *exordium*] Latin term for the beginning of a discourse; common rhetorical exercise in English grammar schools, and therefore appropriate to men, not women.

several] various.

127. *knit . . . after*] spend the rest of my life knitting (a woman's traditional pastime, but also alluding to the female destinies who knit the length of a person's life).

129. *look before you*] i.e., look to the future.

131. *imputation*] accusation.

132. *shows*] appears.

Livia. Weigh but the person, and the hopes you have
      To work this desperate cure.
Maria.   A weaker subject   135
      Would shame the end I aim at. Disobedience?
      You talk too tamely. By the faith I have
      In mine own noble will, that childish woman
      That lives a prisoner to her husband's pleasure
      Has lost her making, and becomes a beast   140
      Created for his use, not fellowship.
Livia. His first wife said as much.
Maria.   She was a fool,
      And took a scurvy course. Let her be named
      'Mongst those that wish for things but dare not do 'em.
      I have a new dance for him, and a mad one.   145
Livia. [*To Bianca*] Are you of this faith?
Bianca.   Yes, truly, and will die in't.
Livia. Why then, let's all wear breeches.
Bianca.   That's a good wench!
Maria. Now thou com'st near the nature of a woman.
      Hang those tame-hearted eyases that no sooner
      See the lure out and hear their husbands holler   150

---

134. *Weigh . . . person*] Consider the person (Petruccio).

hopes] (slender) means.

135. *subject*] i.e., challenge.

140. *making*] true nature.

140–1. *a beast . . . fellowship*] (Alluding to Genesis: the animals were created for Adam's use, but Eve was created as a companion.)

141. *fellowship*] partnership, alliance, intimate friendship, union of equals.

143. *scurvy*] worthless, contemptible. (Scurvy is a disfiguring disease resulting from malnutrition.)

144. *'Mongst*] amongst.

145. *a new dance*] in contrast to Petruccio's 'wooing dance' in Shakespeare's *Shrew*, 1.2.67.

149–59.] Maria here reverses an extended image Shakespeare's Petruccio uses in his soliloquy about 'how to tame a shrew': 'My falcon now is sharp and passing empty, / And till she stoop she shall not be full-gorged, / For then she never looks upon her lure. / Another way I have to man my haggard, / To make her come and know her keeper's call' (*Shrew*, 4.1.176–80).

149. *eyases*] young hawks (compared in *Hamlet* to boy actors, like those who played women's roles).

150. *lure*] apparatus used by falconers to train hawks.

But cry like kites upon 'em! The free haggard
(Which is that woman that has wing and knows it,
Spirit and plume) will make a hundred checks
To show her freedom, sail in every air
And look out every pleasure, not regarding   155
Lure nor quarry till her pitch command
What she desires, making her foundered keeper
Be glad to fling out trains (and golden ones)
To take her down again.
Livia.   You are learnèd, sister.
Yet I say still, take heed.
Maria.   A witty saying!   160
I'll tell thee, Livia: had this fellow tired
As many wives as horses under him,
With spurring of their patience, had he got
A patent, with an office to reclaim us,
Confirmed by Parliament, had he the malice   165
And subtlety of devils or of us

---

151. *kites*] birds of prey, scavengers. (Term of abuse.)

haggard] female adult hawk, full-plumed. (Shakespeare's Hortensio calls Bianca 'this proud disdainful haggard', *Shrew*, 4.2.39.)

153. *Spirit*] (1) vitality; (2) courage; (3) intelligence; (4) wind (under her wings).

plume] full plumage; but also suggesting the crest of a (male) soldier's helmet.

checks] (1) stoopings at game other than the prey her keeper wants her to attack; (2) taunts; (3) rebukes.

156. *quarry*] bird flown at by a hawk.

pitch] (1) height to which a falcon soars before swooping down on its prey; (2) fixed opinion; (3) register of voice.

157. *foundered*] (1) disabled, lamed; (2) stuck in the mire; (3) sent to the bottom (from the perspective of the bird, high above).

keeper] (1) gamekeeper; (2) guardian, husband; (3) man who keeps a mistress.

158. *trains*] (1) pieces of meat laid in a line to lure falcons to their keepers; (2) elongated parts of skirts trailing behind on the ground, worn by women of rank; (3) groups of attendants waiting on a person of importance.

159. *take her down*] (1) make the bird descend; (2) persuade a woman to lie down for sexual intercourse.

162. *horses*] (See introduction, pp. 16–23.)

164. *patent*] licence, monopoly.

office] commission.

166. *or*] either.

Or anything that's worse than both –
Livia. Hey, hey, boys! This is excellent.
Maria.   Or could he
    Cast his wives new again, like bells, to make 'em
    Sound to his will, or had the fearful name   170
    Of the first breaker of wild women, yet,
    Yet would I undertake this man, thus single,
    And spite of all the freedom he has reached to
    Turn him and bend him as I list, and mould him
    Into a babe again, that agèd women,   175
    Wanting both teeth and spleen, may master him.
Bianca. Thou wilt be chronicled.
Maria.   That's all I aim at.
Livia. I must confess I do with all my heart
    Hate an imperious husband, and in time
    Might be so wrought upon –
Bianca.   To make him cuckold?   180
Maria. If he deserve it.
Livia.   There I'll leave ye, ladies.
Bianca. Thou hast not so much noble anger in thee.
Maria. Go sleep, go sleep. What we intend to do
    Lies not for such starved souls as thou hast, Livia.
Livia. Good night. The bridegroom will be with you
        presently.   185
Maria. That's more than you know.
Livia.   If ye work upon him
    As ye have promised, ye may give example,

---

168. *boys*] (1) Probably mimicking male slang, and comparing Maria and
Bianca to 'roaring boys', groups of males who specialized in braggadocio;
(2) adolescent male actors, playing the roles of Maria and Bianca.
    169. *Cast*] make in a mould with molten metal.
    170. *fearful name*] fearsome reputation.
    172. *undertake*] take on.
    single] single-handed.
    173. *spite of*] in spite of.
    reached to] attained.
    174. *list*] wish.
    176. *Wanting*] lacking.
    spleen] bodily organ associated with irritable moods and aggression.
    177. *be chronicled*] make history.
    180. *wrought*] prevailed.
    187. *give example*] set an example.

Which no doubt will be followed.

Maria.   So.

Bianca. Good night. We'll trouble you no further.

Maria. If you intend no good, pray do no harm.   190

Livia. None, but pray for ye.   *Exit Livia.*

Maria.   Now, Bianca –

Bianca.   Cheer, wench!

Maria. Those wits we have, let's wind 'em to the height.

My rest is up, wench, and I pull for that

Will make me ever famous. They that lay

Foundations are half-builders, all men say.   195

Enter JAQUES.

Jaques. My master, forsooth –

Maria.   Oh, how does *thy* master?

Prithee, commend me to him.

Jaques. [*Aside*]   How is this? –

My master stays, forsooth –

Maria.   Why, let him stay.

Who hinders him, forsooth?

Jaques. [*Aside*]   The revel's ended now. –

To visit you.

Maria.   I am not sick.

Jaques.   I mean,   200

To see his chamber, forsooth.

Maria.   Am I his groom?

---

193. *rest is up*] stake is laid.

pull] draw a card.

that] that which.

196. *forsooth*] truly. (A mild oath, sarcastically repeated by Maria.)

thy] (Maria emphasizes the fact that Petruccio is Jacques' master, not hers.)

198. *stays*] waits.

199. *revel's ended*] party's over.

200. *visit*] (Maria takes this in the specific sense 'attend on a sick person'.)

201. *his chamber*] Jaques later explains this phrase: 'I mean, *your* chamber' (l.204): Petruccio expects to consummate his marriage in his bride's bedroom. Maria objects to the appropriation (by which her space has suddenly become 'his').

groom] male attendant, one who would help him to bed.

Where lay he last night, forsooth?
Jaques.   In the low matted parlour.
Maria. There lies his way, by the long gallery.
Jaques. I mean, *your* chamber. You're very merry, mistress.
Maria. 'Tis a good sign I am sound-hearted, Jaques.   205
 But, if you'll know where I lie, follow me,
 And what thou see'st deliver to thy master.
Bianca. Do, gentle Jaques.   *Exeunt* MARIA *and* BIANCA.
Jaques.   Ha, is the wind in that door?
 By'r Lady, we shall have foul weather, then.
 I do not like the shuffling of these women.   210
 They are mad beasts when they knock their heads
  together.
 I have observed 'em all this day: their whispers
 One in another's ear, their signs and pinches,
 And breaking often into violent laughters,
 As if the end they purposed were their own.   215
 Call you these weddings? Sure, this is a knavery,
 A very rank and dainty knavery,
 Marvellous finely carried, that's the comfort.
 What would these women do in ways of honour
 That are such masters this way? Well, my sir   220
 Has been as good at finding out these toys
 As any living. If he lose it now,
 At his own peril be it! I must follow.   *Exit.*

---

202. *low*] (1) downstairs; (2) low-ceilinged; (3) inferior.
matted] with coarse pleated material strewn on the floor (where he presumably slept).
parlour] small private room.
203. *gallery*] corridor.
207. *deliver*] report.
208. *wind . . . door*] (Proverbial. 'Door' means 'direction, quarter'.)
209. *By'r Lady*] An oath: 'By our Lady', the Virgin Mary.
210. *shuffling*] (1) manner of walking; (2) mixing and dealing of cards; (3) joining together; (4) sneaky behaviour.
211. *knock*] put.
215.] as if they were keeping their plans to themselves, i.e., conspiring together.
217. *rank*] fertile, luxurious, licentious, gross, rancid.
dainty] rare, delicate, fastidious, excellent.
221. *toys*] tricks.

1.3

Enter Servants *with lights,* PETRUCCIO, PETRONIUS, MOROSO,
TRANIO, *and* SOPHOCLES.

Petruccio. You that are married, gentlemen, have at ye
  For a round wager now.
Sophocles.   Of this night's stage?
Petruccio. Yes.
Sophocles.   I am your first man.
  A pair of gloves of twenty shillings.
Petruccio.   Done.
  Who takes me up else? I am for all bets.   5
Moroso. Faith, lusty Lawrence, were but my night now,
  Old as I am I would make you clap on spurs
  But I would reach you, and bring you to your trot too.
  I would, gallant.
Petruccio. Well said, Good-will. But where's the stuff, boy, eh?   10
  Old father Time, your hourglass is empty.
Petronius. [*To Moroso*] See how these boys despise us? –
  Well, son, well,

1.3] Petronius's house.

0.1 with lights] (indicating that night has fallen).

1. *married*] already married (not newly married).

have at ye] I challenge you.

2. *round*] sizeable.

wager] (The men bet on Petruccio's sexual performance.)

stage] (1) as much of a journey as is performed without stopping for rest;
(2) performance space, theatre.

3. *first man*] first to take the bet.

6. *Faith*] In faith. (A mild oath.)

lusty Lawrence] (Lecherous friar of folktales; both this and 'Good-will' in
line 10 allude to the Robin Hood legend.)

were . . . now] if only this were my night to get married.

7. *clap on spurs*] (Continuing the metaphor of a journey on horseback,
combined with the equestrian image of sexual riding.)

8. *bring . . . trot*] (1) get your horse trotting; (2) bring you to your female
horse, nag.

10. *Good-will*] 'Mr Good Intentions' (sarcastic).

stuff] (1) provisions, materials, inward capabilities; (2) semen.

boy] (Old men are often compared to prepubertal children.)

11. *hourglass*] i.e., scrotum.

12. *son*] son-in-law.

This pride will have a fall.
Petruccio.   Upon your daughter.
But I shall rise again, if there be truth
In – eggs and buttered parsnips.   15
Petronius. Will you to bed, son, and leave talking?
Tomorrow morning we shall have you look,
For all your great words, like St George at Kingston,
Running a-footback from the furious dragon,
That with her angry tail belabours him   20
For being lazy.
Sophocles.   His warlike lance
Bent like a crossbow lath, alas the while!
Tranio. His courage quenched, and so far quenched –
Petruccio.   'Tis well, sir.
Tranio. That any privy saint, even small St Davy,
May lash him with a leek.
Petruccio.   What then?
Sophocles.   ' "Fly, fly!" quoth then   25
The fearful dwarf; "here is no place for living men." '

---

13. *pride . . . fall*] (Proverbial.)

14. *rise*] have an erection. (But blasphemously suggesting the resurrection of Christ.)

15. *eggs . . . parsnips*] (Where we expect Petruccio to invoke the truth of Scripture, he instead speaks of conventional aphrodisiacs.)

16. *leave*] stop.

18. *St George*] the patron saint of England, here painted on an inn sign, not defeating but fleeing the (female) dragon.

Kingston] village north of London (first clear indication that the play is set in England).

19. *a-footback*] on foot (joking on the fact that a knight should be 'a-horseback').

20. *tail*] (1) dragon's tail; (2) woman's genitals, angry because sexually unsatisfied.

21. *lance*] (1) weapon used in jousting; (2) penis.

22. *lath*] the part of the crossbow which bends when drawn.

23. *courage*] (1) bravery; (2) sexual potency.

24. *privy*] (1) private; (2) native; (3) latrine; (4) associated with the genitals.

small] short. (Conventional attribute of Welshmen.)

St Davy] patron saint of Wales.

25. *leek*] vegetable associated with Wales.

25–6.] (Quoting Edmund Spenser's *Faerie Queene.* 1.1.13.8–9, of running away from a female dragon.)

26. *dwarf*] (Suggesting diminutive sexual stature.)

Petruccio. Well, my masters, if I do sink under my business, as
    I find 'tis very possible, I am not the first that has
    miscarried so. That's my comfort. What may be done
    without impeach or waste, I can and will do.   30

               Enter JAQUES.

    How now! Is my fair bride a-bed?
Jaques. No, truly, sir.
Petronius. Not a-bed yet?
    Body o' me, we'll up and rifle her.
    Here's a coil with a maidenhead! 'Tis not entailed, is it?   35
Petruccio. If it be, I'll try all the law i'th' land but I'll cut
    it off.
    Let's up, let's up, come.
Jaques.   That you cannot, neither.
Petruccio. Why?
Jaques. Unless you'll drop through the chimney like a daw or   40
    force a breach i'th' windows.
    You may untile the house; 'tis possible.
Petruccio. What dost thou mean?
Jaques. A moral, sir. The ballad will express it.
    [*Sings*] The wind and the rain   45
    Has turned you back again.
    Ye cannot be lodged there. –
    The truth is, all the doors are barricaded.
    Not a cat-hole but holds a murd'rer in't.

---

   27. *masters*] (A term of respect: sirs.)

   30. *impeach*] injury.

   34. *Body o' me*] (An oath, originally referring to the Body of Christ.)
rifle] rouse.

   35. *coil*] fuss.

entailed] A pun on real estate held in trust ('entailed'), here alluding to
the bride's 'tail'.

   36–7. *cut it off*] (1) repossess the 'entailed' land; (2) cut off her 'tail' or
maidenhead (i.e., break the hymen).

   38. *Let's*] Let's go.

   40. *daw*] jackdaw, a small bird.

   48. *barricaded*] Maria's action literalizes a classic Petrarchan trope: the
woman's body is imagined as a walled city, which a male besieges; when she
surrenders, he enters.

   49. *cat-hole*] hole for letting a cat into the house.
murd'rer] A 'murderer' was a small cannon.

She's victualled for this month.

Petruccio.   Art thou not drunk?   50

Sophocles. He's drunk, he's drunk. Come, come, let's up.

Jaques.   Yes, yes,

I am drunk. Ye may go up, ye may, gentlemen,

But take heed to your heads. I say no more.

Sophocles. I'll try that.   *Exit.*

Petronius. How dost thou say? The door fast locked, fellow?   55

Jaques. Yes, truly, sir, 'tis locked, and guarded too,

And two as desperate tongues planted behind it

As e'er yet battered.

They stand upon their honours and will not give up
without strange composition, I will assure you. Marching   60
away with their pieces cocked, and bullets in their
mouths, will not satisfy them.

Petruccio. How's this? How's this? *They* are? Is there another
with her?

Jaques. Yes, marry, is there, and an engineer.

Moroso. Who's that, for [God's] sake?   65

Jaques. Colonel Bianca. She commands the works.

Spinola's but a ditcher to her. There's a half-moon (I am
but a poor man, but if you'd give me leave, sir, I'll venture
a year's wages), draw all your force before it

And mount your ablest piece of battery,   70

---

50. *victualled*] provisioned, as a city prepared for siege.

57. *tongues*] (Punning on 'tongs', compared to battering rams.)

60. *composition*] negotiated settlement.

61. *pieces*] guns.

cocked] with the cock pulled back, ready for firing when the trigger is pulled (but 'cock' was also slang for 'penis').

61–2. *their mouths*] (A deliberate conflation of the mouths of the guns and of the women).

64. *marry*] A weak interjection (originally 'by Mary').

engineer] designer of military machines and fortifications.

66. *works*] earthworks, defences.

67. *Spinola*] Spinola was a famous Italian general who commanded the Spanish army when it captured Ostend in the Netherlands in 1604.

but a ditcher] only a ditch-digger.

half-moon] (1) semi-circular defensive fortification; (2) crescent-shaped outline of a woman's genitals.

70. *piece of battery*] battering ram. (With continuing metaphor of a penis attempting forcible entry.)

You shall not enter in't these three nights yet.
Petruccio. I should laugh at that, good Jaques.

Enter SOPHOCLES.

Sophocles. Beat back again! She's fortified for ever.
Jaques. Am I drunk now, sir?
Sophocles. He that dares most, go up now and be cooled.   75
    I have scaped a pretty scouring.
Petruccio. What, are they mad? Have we another bedlam?
    She doth not talk, I hope.
Sophocles. Oh, terribly, extremely, fearfully.
    The noise at London Bridge is nothing near her.   80
Petruccio. How got she tongue?
Sophocles.   As you got tail: she was born to't.
Petruccio. Locked out o' doors, and on my wedding night?
    Nay, an I suffer this, I may go graze.
    Come, gentlemen, I'll batter. Are these virtues?
Sophocles. Do, and be beaten off with shame, as I was.   85
    I went up, came to th' door, knocked, nobody answered,
    Knocked louder, yet heard nothing, would have broke in
    By force, when suddenly a waterwork
    Flew from the window with such violence
    That had I not ducked quickly like a friar,   90
    Caetera quis nescit?
    The chamber's nothing but a mere Ostend,

---

75. *cooled*] (Both literally, by the contents of the chamber pots described below in line 88, and figuratively.)

76. *scaped*] barely escaped.

77. *bedlam*] insane asylum (referring to London's St Bethlehem's hospital.)

80. *noise*] (Caused by the tide rushing through the arches.)

81. *tail*] penis. (Emblematic organ of males, as 'tongue' is the emblematic organ of females.)

83. *an*] if.
I . . . graze] put me out to pasture.

88. *waterwork*] (1) fountain; (2) stream of urine.

91. Caetera quis nescit?] Who knows what would have happened next? (Friars used Latin and were satirized for excessive 'ducking' or bowing and genuflecting.)

92. *Ostend*] Protestant city in the Netherlands long besieged by the Catholic Spanish.

In every window pewter cannons mounted.
You'll quickly find with what they are charged, sir.
Petruccio. Why then, tantara for us!   95
Sophocles. And all the lower works lined sure with small shot,
    Long tongues with firelocks, that, at twelve-score blank,
    Hit to the heart. Now, an ye dare, go up.

        Enter MARIA *and* BIANCA *above* [*at a window*].

Moroso. The window opens. Beat a parley first.
    I am so much amazed, my very hair stands.   100
Petronius. Why, how now, daughter? What, entrenched?
Maria. A little guarded for my safety, sir.
Petruccio. For your safety, sweetheart? Why, who offends you?
    I come not to use violence.
Maria.   I think
    You cannot, sir. I am better fortified.   105
Petruccio. I know your end: you would fain reprieve your
        maidenhead
    A night or two.
Maria. Yes – or ten, or twenty, sir, or say a hundred,
    Or indeed till I list lie with you.
Sophocles. That's a shrewd saying. From this present hour   110

---

93. *pewter cannons*] chamber-pots mounted as weapons.

94. *charged*] loaded.

95. *tantara*] Onamatopoetic term for a flourish of trumpets, here summoning the men to battle.

96. *lower works*] (1) earthworks or battlements; (2) lower windows of the house.

small shot] musket bullets, as distinct from cannon-balls.

97. *Long tongues*] (1) long-winded speakers; (2) projections of a fortification; (3) long clappers of bells.

firelocks] mechanisms for igniting the charge in a gun (but also suggesting 'fiery locks' or hair).

twelve-score blank] 240 feet range.

98. *Hit to the heart*] (1) fatally wound; (2) emotionally wound.

98.1. above] Maria's bedroom is on an upper storey, facing the inner courtyard of her father's house. But for an audience this is indistinguishable from her occupying the whole house, and the men standing in the street outside it.

99. *Beat a parley*] Beat drums as a signal requesting the right to approach and talk to an enemy army.

109. *list*] wish to.

110. *shrewd*] shrewish.

I never will believe a 'silent woman';
When they break out they are bonfires.
Petronius. [*To Maria*] Till you list lie with him? Why, who
    are you, madam?
Bianca. That trim gentleman's wife, sir.
Petruccio.   Cry ye mercy!
    Do ye command too?
Maria.   Yes, marry, does she, and in chief.   115
Bianca. I do command, and you shall go without
    (I mean your wife) for this night.
Maria. And for the next too, wench, and so as't follows.
Petronius. Thou wilt not, wilt 'a?
Maria.   Yes, indeed, dear father,
    And till he seals to what I shall set down,   120
    For anything I know, for ever.
Sophocles.   By'r Lady,
    These are bug's words.
Tranio. [*To Petruccio*]   You hear her, sir, she *can* talk,
    God be thanked.
Petruccio.   I would I heard it not, sir.
Sophocles. I find that all the pity bestowed upon this woman
    Makes but an anagram of 'an ill wife',   125
    For she was never virtuous.
Petruccio. [*To Maria*] You'll let me in, I hope, for all this
    jesting.

---

111. *'silent woman'*] (Alluding to the alternative title and title character of
Ben Jonson's play *Epicene*, probably performed by the same acting company
at about the same time.)

114. *trim*] fine, nice, cute. (With irony.)
Cry ye mercy] I beg your pardon.

119. *wilt 'a*] will you.

120. *seals*] indicates his acceptance, by affixing his seal (to a document).
set] write.

122. *bug's words*] the words of a bugbear, an object of terror.

125. *anagram*] transposition of letters, creating a different word or phrase
(a widely practised and respected literary device in the Renaissance).

'an ill wife'] anagram of 'a fine will'. A bad wife is a woman who has a
'fine' (egregious, keen-edged, artful, overly fastidious; the word is often used
sarcastically) 'will' (disposition, determination, stubbornness, whim, sexual
appetite). These bad qualities are only encouraged by 'all the pity bestowed'
on her: sympathy spoils a woman.

126. *virtuous*] good natured; gracious; chaste.

127. *for*] despite.

Maria. Hope still, sir.
Petronius.   You will come down, I am sure.
Maria. I am sure I will not.
Petronius.   I'll fetch you then.
Bianca. The power of the whole country cannot, sir,   130
    Unless we please to yield – which yet I think we shall not.
    Charge when you please, you shall hear quickly from us.
Moroso. [God] bless me from a chicken of thy hatching!
    Is this wiving?
Petruccio. Prithee, Maria, tell me what's the reason –   135
    And do it freely – you deal thus strangely with me?
    You were not forced to marry; your consent
    Went equally with mine, if not before it.
    I hope you do not doubt I want that mettle
    A man should have to keep a woman waking;   140
    I would be sorry to be such a saint yet.
    My person, as it is not excellent,
    So 'tis not old, or lame, or weak with physic,
    But well enough to please an honest woman
    That keeps her house and loves her husband.
Maria.   'Tis so.   145
Petruccio. My means and my conditions are no shamers
    Of him that owns 'em – all the world knows that –
    And my friends no reliers on my fortunes.
Maria. All this I believe, and none of all these parcels
    I dare except against; nay more, so far   150
    I am from making these the ends I aim at,
    These idle outward things, these woman's fears,

---

133. *bless*] shield.
134. *chicken . . . hatching*] i.e., child of yours.
139. *doubt*] fear.
    mettle] spirit; sexual capability.
140. *waking*] awake (in bed). The phrase 'keep the (widow, wife, wench) waking' was often used in reference to a man's sexual endurance.
142. *person*] personal appearance, body.
143. *with physic*] by medical treatment, particularly purging and bleeding.
144. *honest*] trustworthy; chaste.
146. *conditions*] qualities.
148. *friends*] relatives.
149. *parcels*] particulars, items in a legal document.
150. *except against*] take exception to.

That, were I yet unmarried, free to choose
Through all the tribes of man, I'd take Petruccio
In's shirt, with one ten groats to pay the priest,   155
Before the best man living, or the ablest
That e'er leaped out of Lancashire – and they are right
    ones.

Petronius. Why do you play the fool then, and stand prating
Out of the window, like a broken miller?

Petruccio. If you will have me credit you, Maria,   160
Come down and let your love confirm it.

Maria.   Stay there, sir.
That bargain's yet to make.

Bianca.   Play sure, wench.
The pack's in thine own hand.

Sophocles.   Let me die lousy
If these two wenches be not brewing knavery
To stock a kingdom.

Petruccio.   'Death, this is a riddle: 165
'I love ye, and I love ye not.'

Maria.   It is so,
And till your own experience do untie it,
This distance I must keep.

Petruccio.   If you talk more,
I am angry, very angry.

Maria. I am glad on't, and I *will* talk.

Petruccio.   Prithee, peace.   170
Let me not think thou art mad. I tell thee, woman,

---

155. *groats*] coins equal to four pence.

157. *leaped*] (Punning on 'sexually mounted'.)

Lancashire] English county celebrated for its prowess in fencing.

159. *broken*] bankrupt.

miller] Proverbially dishonest; also proverbially, 'he is a loud speaker, who is brought up in a mill'.

161. *Stay there*] Stop on that point.

163. *pack's*] deck of cards is.

lousy] infested with lice.

164. *knavery*] dishonest tricks (imagined as ale or beer, perhaps by association with the herb 'knavery' = bog asphodel).

165. *To stock*] sufficient to stock.

'Death] Truncated form of 'God's death' (an oath).

170. *on't*] of it.

If thou go'st forward, I am still Petruccio.
Maria. And I am worse: a woman that can fear
    Neither Petruccio Furius, nor his fame,
    Nor anything that tends to our allegiance.   175
    There's a short method for ye; now you know me.
Petruccio. If you can carry't so, 'tis very well.
Bianca. No, you shall carry it, sir.
Petruccio.   Peace, gentle low-bell.
Petronius. [*To Maria*] Use no more words, but come down
    instantly.
    I charge thee, by the duty of a child.   180
Petruccio. Prithee, come, Maria. I forgive all.
Maria. [*To Petronius*] Stay there. That duty that you charge
    me by –
    If you consider truly what you say –
    Is now another man's; you gave't away
    I'th' church, if you remember, to my husband.   185
    So all you can exact now is no more
    But only a due reverence to your person,
    Which thus I pay: your blessing, and I am gone
    To bed for this night.
Petronius.   This is monstrous.
    That blessing that St Dunstan gave the devil,   190
    If I were near thee, I would give thee –
    Pull thee down by th' nose!
Bianca.   Saints should not rave, sir.

---

174. *Petruccio Furius*] Allusion to Orlando Furioso, the Italian hero of
Ariosto's Renaissance epic poem, translated by Harington (1591, 1607); also
the hero of an anonymous Elizabethan play, Orlando was driven mad by a
woman's infidelity.

176. *method*] orderly exposition, table of contents.

177. *carry't*] carry it off. (But Bianca parries this by treating the phrase
as though it meant 'put up with it'.)

178. *low-bell*] This may mean bell-wether or bell-wearing animal leading
a flock, or a bell used at night to stupefy birds so that they can be easily
caught.

180. *of a child*] that a child owes its parent.

188. *your blessing*] give me your blessing.

190. *St Dunstan*] Archbishop of Canterbury 960–88; when tempted by a
devil in the form of a woman, he seized her by the nose with red-hot tongs.

A little rhubarb now were excellent.

Petruccio. Then, by that duty you owe *me*, Maria,
　　Open the door and be obedient. I am quiet yet.　　195

Maria. I do confess that duty. Make your best on't.

Petruccio. Why, give me leave, I will.

Bianca.　　　　　　　　　　　Sir, there's no learning
　　An old stiff jade to trot. You know the moral.

Maria. [*To Petruccio*] Yet, as I take it, sir, I owe no more
　　Than you owe back again.

Petruccio.　　　　　　　You will not article?　　200
　　All I owe, presently – let me but up – I'll pay.

Maria. You're too hot, and such prove jades at length.
　　You do confess a duty or respect
　　To me from you again that's very near
　　Or full the same with mine?

Petruccio.　　　　　　　Yes.　　205

Maria. Then by that duty or respect or what
　　You please to have it, go to bed and leave me
　　And trouble me no longer with your fooling;
　　For know, I am not for you.

Petruccio. [*To the men*]　　　Well, what remedy?

Petronius. A fine smart cudgel. – Oh, that I were near thee!　　210

Bianca. If you had teeth now, what a case were we in!

Moroso. These are the most authentic rebels, next
　　Tyrone, I ever read of.

Maria. [*To Petruccio*] A week hence, or a fortnight, as you
　　bear ye
　　And as I find my will observed, I may,　　215
　　With intercession of some friends, be brought,

---

193. *rhubarb*] (Used as a laxative; purgation was believed to have psychological as well as physical benefits.)

194. me] (As opposed to her father.)

197. *learning*] teaching.

198. *jade*] (1) old or ill-spirited horse; (2) woman. (Contemptuous.)

200. *article*] stipulate particulars of a treaty.

201. owe] According to the Christian notion of 'conjugal debt', a husband owes his wife regular sexual intercourse.

up] (1) come upstairs; (2) get an erection.

213. *Tyrone*] Hugh O'Neill, Earl of Tyrone, leader (1595–1614) of Irish resistance to English occupation.

214. *bear ye*] conduct yourself.

May be, to kiss you, and so quarterly
To pay a little rent by composition.
You understand me?

Sophocles.   Thou boy, thou!

Petruccio.   Well,
There are more maids than Maudlin; that's my comfort.   220

Maria. Yes, and more men than Michael.

Petruccio.   I must not
To bed with this stomach, and no meat, lady.

Maria. Feed where you will, so it be sound and wholesome;
Else live at livery, for I'll none with ye.

Bianca. [*To Petruccio*] You had best back one of the dairy
    maids; they'll carry.   225
But take heed to your girths; you'll get a bruise else.

Petruccio. Now, if thou wouldst come down, and tender me
All the delights due to a marriage bed,
Study such kisses as would melt a man,
And turn thyself into a thousand figures   230
To add new flames unto me, I would stand
Thus heavy, thus regardless, thus despising
Thee and thy best allurings. All the beauty
That's laid upon your bodies, mark me well –
For without doubt your minds are miserable;   235

---

218. *composition*] agreement by which a creditor accepts a certain portion of a debt.

219. *boy*] (He calls her a boy because she's not acting womanly.)

220. *There . . . Maudlin*] (Proverbial.)

222. *stomach*] appetite (here, sexual).

meat] sexual flesh. (But playing on the sense 'supper'.)

223. *so*] provided.

224. *at livery*] (of a horse) kept for the owner, and fed and groomed at a fixed charge.

225. *back*] mount.

carry] (usually milk pails, but here a man).

226. *girths*] belt tied around body of a horse, to secure the saddle (implying that Petruccio may be thrown off his mount, otherwise).

227. *if*] even if.

230. *figures*] (1) sexual positions; (2) rhetorical tropes used for persuasion, seduction.

232. *heavy*] unmoved.

regardless] impervious.

234. *your*] (Referring to women generally.)

You have no masks for them – all this rare beauty,
Lay but the painter and the silk-worm by,
The doctor with his diets, and the tailor,
And you appear like flayed cats; not so handsome.

Maria. And we appear – like her that sent us hither,   240
That only excellent and beauteous Nature –
Truly ourselves, for men to wonder at,
But too divine to handle. We are gold,
In our own natures pure; but when we suffer
The husband's stamp upon us, then alloys,   245
And base ones, of you men, are mingled with us,
And make us blush like copper.

Petruccio.   Then, and never
Till then, are women to be spoken of,
For till that time you have no souls, I take it.
Good night. – Come, gentlemen, I'll fast for this night.   250
But, by this hand – well, I shall come up yet?

Maria. No.

Petruccio. Then will I watch thee like a withered Jewry.
Thou shalt neither have meat, fire, nor candle,

---

236. *masks*] face masks, worn by upper-class women to protect their complexions (but also for the sake of modesty, like Islamic veils).

237. *painter*] cosmetician.

239. *flayed cats*] (1) felines, flayed because their fur was used as human clothing; (2) undressed prostitutes.

245. *stamp*] physical impression, formed by pressing something hard into something soft; sexual penetration is like the stamping of metal with an image of the sovereign, which makes it legal tender.

alloys] cheap metals mixed with gold (to make it usable as coinage). English currency was debased, by adding more alloys, in July 1605 and November 1611.

249. *no souls*] (A position seriously maintained by some Christian theologians.)

253. *withered*] debilitated (like the victims of a siege), but also old, ugly, physically handicapped or partially paralysed. (Women accused of witch craft were often called 'whithered'.)

Jewry] Jewish ghetto, locked and guarded at night to prevent exit, but also suggesting the famous Roman siege of Jerusalem, in which thousands of rebels died of starvation. (Jews and women were subject to similar prejudices and hostilities.)

254. *meat*] food of any kind. (Jews were accused of cannibalism.)

fire, nor candle] warmth, nor light.

Nor anything that's easy. Do you rebel so soon?				255
	Yet take mercy.
Bianca. Put up your pipes. To bed, sir. I'll assure you
	A month's siege will not shake us.
Moroso.					Well said, colonel.
Maria. To bed, to bed, Petruccio. – Good night, gentlemen.
	You'll make my father sick with sitting up.				260
	Here you shall find us any time these ten days,
	Unless we may march off with our contentment.
Petruccio. I'll hang first.
Maria.				And I'll quarter, if I do not.
	I'll make ye know, and fear, a wife, Petruccio;
	There lies my cause.								265
	You have been famous for a woman-tamer
	And bear the feared name of a brave wife-breaker;
	A woman now shall take those honours off, and tame
		you.
	Nay, never look so big; she shall, believe me,
	And I am she. What think ye? Good night to all.			270
	Ye shall find sentinels –
Bianca.				If ye dare sally.
					Exeunt [BIANCA *and* MARIA] *above.*
Petronius. The devil's in 'em, even the very devil,
	The downright devil!
Petruccio. I'll devil 'em. By these ten bones, I will.
	I'll bring it to th' old proverb: 'No sport, no pie.'			275

---

255. *easy*] comfortable.
  rebel] (Jews were accused of rebellion against the Romans and against Christ, and said to have no allegiances to their modern sovereigns.)
  256. *take*] accept (my offer of).
  257. *Put . . . pipes*] give it up. (Proverbial, but also punning on *pipe* as 'penis'.)
  258. *Well said, colonel*] (Said sardonically.)
  262. *with our contentment*] without being interfered with.
  263. *I'll quarter*] (1) I'll stay at home; (2) I'll provide lodgings for soldiers; (3) I'll be cut like a criminal's body into four parts (as in the phrase 'hanged, drawn, and quartered').
  269. *big*] threatening.
  271. *sally*] venture out to attack.
  274. *ten bones*] i.e., ten fingers (two fists).
  275. *sport*] (1) sex; (2) entertainment. (The modern athletic sense is anachronistic.)

'Death, taken down i'th' top of all my speed!
This is fine dancing! Gentlemen, stick to me.
You see our freehold's touched, and, by this light,
We will beleaguer 'em, and either starve 'em out
Or make 'em recreant.   280
Petronius. I'll see all passages stopped but these about 'em.
If the good women of the town dare succour 'em,
We shall have wars indeed.
Sophocles.   I'll stand *perdu* upon 'em.
Moroso. My regiment shall lie before.
Jaques. I think so: 'tis grown too old to stand.   285
Petruccio. Let's in, and each provide him to his tackle.
We'll fire 'em out, or make 'em take their pardons –
Hear what I say – on their bare knees. ['Od's precious!]
Am I Petruccio, feared and spoken of,
And on my wedding night am I thus jaded?   *Exeunt.*   290

1.4

Enter ROLAND *at one door,* PEDRO *hastily at the other.*

Roland. Now, Pedro!
Pedro.   Very busy, Master Roland.
Roland. What haste, man?
Pedro.   I beseech you, pardon me,

---

276. *'Death*] God's death. (A strong oath.)

278. *freehold's*] property or office held in perpetuity (here, the status of
husband) is.

touched] endangered, affected.

280. *recreant*] (1) avowedly defeated; (2) apostate to their religion.

281. *passages . . . 'em*] passageways except the upper balcony and
windows (which the women control.)

283. *stand perdu*] keep watch.

285. *stand*] have an erection (punning on 'lie', line 284).

286. *tackle*] weapons; instruments of war (also suggesting a man's sexual
'weapon').

288. *Od's precious*] by God's precious body (a strong oath).

290. *jaded*] (1) tricked; (2) made a fool of; (3) turned into a horse for
someone else to ride (when he should be the rider).

1.4] Petronius's house.

I am not mine own man.
Roland.   Thou art not mad?
Pedro. No, but believe me, as hasty.
Roland.   The cause, good Pedro?
Pedro. There be a thousand, sir. You are not married?   5
Roland. Not yet.
Pedro.   Keep yourself quiet, then.
Roland.   Why?
Pedro. You'll find a fiddle that never will be tuned else.
    From all such women, [Lord] deliver me!   *Exit* PEDRO.
Roland. What ails the fellow, trow?

Enter JAQUES.

                              Jaques!
Jaques.   Your friend, sir;
    But very full of business.
Roland.   Nothing but business!   10
    Prithee, thy reason? Is there any dying?
Jaques. I would there were, sir.
Roland.   But thy business?
Jaques. I'll tell you in a word: I am sent to lay
    An imposition upon souse and puddings,
    Pasties and penny custards, that the women   15
    May not relieve yon rebels. Fare ye well, sir.
Roland. How does thy mistress?
Jaques.   Like a resty jade:
    She's spoiled for riding.   *Exit.*
Roland.   What a devil ail they?

---

3. *not . . . man*] at another's command.
7. *fiddle . . . tuned*] i.e., woman or sex organ that will not be mastered or made fit for 'playing' (sex).
9. *trow?*] do you suppose?
12. *would*] wish.
14. *imposition*] boycott.
souse] part of a pig or other animal, pickled.
14. *puddings*] (1) sausages; (2) puddings.
15. *Pasties*] meat pies.
penny] (Price of admission to the Globe theatre.)
custards] (1) quiche with meat; (2) egg-based dessert.
17. *resty*] restless.
18. *What . . . they?*] What the devil is wrong with them?

Custards and penny pasties, fools and fiddles?
What's this to th' purpose?

Enter SOPHOCLES.

Oh, well met!
Sophocles.   Now, Roland!   20
    I cannot stay to talk long.
Roland.   What's the matter?
    Here's stirring, but to what end? Whither go you?
Sophocles. To view the works.
Roland.   What works?
Sophocles.   The women's trenches.
Roland. Trenches? Are such to see?
Sophocles.   I do not jest, sir.
Roland. I cannot understand you.
Sophocles.   Do not you hear   25
    In what a state of quarrel the new bride
    Stands with her husband?
Roland.   Let him stand with her,
    And there's an end.
Sophocles.   It should be, but, by'r Lady,
    She holds him out at pike's end, and defies him,
    And now is fortified. Such a regiment of rutters   30
    Never defied men braver. I am sent
    To view their preparation.
Roland.   This is news
    Stranger than armies in the air. You saw not
    My gentle mistress?
Sophocles.   Yes, and meditating

---

23. *works*] fortifications. (But the word has many other meanings; hence
Roland's confusion.)

trenches] defensive excavations. (But Roland takes it to mean 'genitals':
compare 'cut' or 'slit'.)

24. *to see*] to be seen.

27. *stand*] get an erection.

29. *pike's end*] the end of her lance or his penis.

30. *rutters*] (1) cavalry soldiers (specifically German soldiers); (2) animals
in heat.

33. *armies in the air*] ominous meteorological phenomena.

34. *gentle*] well-born.

Upon some secret business. When she had found it,					35
She leaped for joy, and laughed, and straight retired
To shun Moroso.
Roland.					This may be, for me.
Sophocles. Will you along?
Roland.					No.
Sophocles.					Fare you well.
Roland.							Farewell, sir.
							Exit SOPHOCLES.
What should her musing mean, and what her joy in't,
If not for my advantage? Stay. May not					40
That bobtail jade Moroso, with his gold,
His gewgaws, and the hope she has to send him
Quickly to dust, excite this?

			Enter LIVIA *at one door, and* MOROSO *at another,*
					as unseen by her, harkening.

					Here she comes,
And yonder walks the stallion to discover.
Yet I'll salute her. – Save you, beauteous mistress.					45
Livia. [*Aside*] The fox is kennelled for me. – Save you, sir.
Roland. Why do you look so strange?
Livia.						I use to look, sir,
Without examination.

---

35. *found it*] figured it out.
36. *straight*] immediately.
37. *for me*] (1) for all I know to the contrary (2) for my benefit.
38. *along*] come along.
40. *Stay*] Wait.
41. *bobtail jade*] (1) nag with its tail cut short; (2) old man with a small penis.
42. *gewgaws*] baubles.
42–3. *the hope . . . dust*] her hope that he will soon die (and leave her his money).
44. *discover*] eaves-drop.
45. *salute*] greet.
Save] God save.
46. *fox*] (Referring to Moroso, whom she sees 'kennelled' or hiding.)
47. *use to*] am accustomed to.

Moroso. [*Aside*] Twenty spur-royals for that word!
Roland.   Belike then
     The object discontents you?
Livia.   Yes, it does.   50
Roland. Is't come to this? You know me, do you not?
Livia. Yes, as I may know many, by repentance.
Roland. Why, do ye break your faith?
Livia.   I'll tell you that too.
     You are under-age, and no bond holds
     Upon you.   55
Moroso. [*Aside*] [God-'a'-mercy] for that, wench!
Livia. Sue out your understanding
     And get more hair to cover your bare knuckle –
     For boys were made for nothing but dry kisses –
     And, if you can, more manners.
Moroso. [*Aside*]   Better still!   60
Livia. And then, if I want Spanish gloves, or stockings,
     A ten-pound waistcoat, or a nag to hunt on,
     It may be I shall grace you to accept 'em.
Roland. Farewell. And when I credit woman more,
     May I to Smithfield, and there buy a jade –   65
     And know him to be so – that breaks my neck.

---

49. *Twenty . . . word*] (Moroso is delighted with Livia's seemingly cold response to Roland; her words are worth their weight in gold. Spur-royals are gold coins so named for the figure of a sun stamped on their reverse, resembling the rowel of a spur.)

Belike] Perhaps.

50. *object*] object of your gaze.

52. *by repentance*] to my sorrow.

54. *under age*] younger than twenty-one, and hence a minor, on whom no 'bond' or contract would hold.

56. *God-'a'-mercy*] Thanks. (Contraction of 'God have mercy upon'.)

57. *Sue out*] Appeal to a court to grant you.

58. *knuckle*] (Maria may be jocularly referring either to Rowland's beardless chin or to his immature genitals. Either way, the point is that he lacks body-hair and hence manliness.)

59. *dry kisses*] i.e., unerotic kisses on cheek or forehead.

60. *manners*] (Punning on 'manors', estates.)

61. *Spanish*] i.e., imported, and of the most highly valued materials.

62. *ten-pound*] i.e., fantastically expensive (equivalent to a teacher's annual salary).

63. *to accept*] by accepting.

65. *Smithfield*] Site of a large fair specializing in sales of horses.

Livia. Because I have known you, I'll be thus kind to you.
    Farewell, and be a man, and I'll provide you,
    Because I see you're desperate, some staid chambermaid
    That may relieve your youth with wholesome doctrine. 70
Moroso. [*Aside*] She's mine from all the world. – Ha, wench!
Livia.   Ha, chicken!
                    She gives him a box o'th' ear, and exit.
Moroso. Is't come to this? – Save you!
Roland.   The devil take you!
                    [*Roland*] *wrings him by th' nose.*
Moroso. Oh!
Roland. There's a love-token for you. Thank me now. *Exit.*
Moroso. I'll think on some of ye. And if I live, 75
    My nose alone shall not be played withal. *Exit.*

---

69. *staid*] steady; stolid.

71. *chicken*] (Perhaps for his wrinkled, loose skin.)

71.1. him] Moroso.

72. *Save you*] (A greeting.)

75. *think*] i.e., plan revenge.

76. *My . . . withal*] (1) My nose is not the only one that will be tortured; (2) My penis is not the only one that will be played with; (3) My nose is not the only part of my body that will be fondled.

Act 2

Enter LIVIA [*with food*], *alone.*

Livia. Now, if I can but get in handsomely,
Father, I shall deceive you, and this night,
For all your private plotting, I'll no wedlock.
I have shifted sail, and find my sister's safety
A sure retirement. Pray to heaven that Roland   5
Believe not too far what I said to him,
For yon old fox-case forced me; that's my fear.
Stay, let me see. This quarter fierce Petruccio
Keeps with his Myrmidons. I must be sudden.
If he seize on me, I can look for nothing   10
But martial law. To this place have I scaped him. –
Above there!

Enter MARIA *and* BIANCA *above at a window.*

Maria.   *Qui va la?*
Livia.   A friend.
Bianca.   Who are you?

2.1] Petronius's house. For the additional scene originally placed here see
Appendix.

1. *in*] i.e., into the women's enclosure.

3. *I'll no*] I'll have no.

4. *shifted sail*] i.e., changed direction.

safety] stronghold.

5. *retirement*] safe place, shelter.

7. *fox-case*] skin of a fox (Moroso).

8. *This quarter*] these quarters, this section of the house (but suggesting
'part of a battlefield').

9. *Myrmidons*] soldiers commanded by Achilles who besieged Troy.
(Livia's point is that she must be 'sudden' in running the men's blockade.)

11. *martial law*] seizure and punishment without trial, in wartime or when
civil liberties have been suspended.

12. Qui va la?] Who goes there?

friend] (1) ally; (2) relative.

Livia. Look out and know.

Maria.   Alas, poor wench, who sent thee?
    What weak fool made thy tongue his orator?
    I know ye come to parley.

Livia.   You're deceived.   15
    Urged by the goodness of your cause, I come
    To do as you do.

Maria.   You're too weak, too foolish,
    To cheat us with your smoothness. Do not we know
    Thou hast been kept up tame?

Livia. Believe me!   20

Maria. No. Prithee, good Livia,
    Utter thy eloquence somewhere else.

Bianca. [*To Livia*]   Good cousin,
    Put up your pipes. We are not for your palate.
    Alas, we know who sent you.

Livia.   O' my faith –

Bianca. Stay there. You must not think 'your faith' or 'troth'   25
    Or 'by your maidenhead' or such Sunday oaths,
    Sworn after evensong, can inveigle us
    To loose our handfast. Did their wisdoms think
    That sent you hither we would be so foolish
    To entertain our gentle sister Sinon   30
    And give her credit, while the wooden jade

---

15. *parley*] negotiate with the enemy.

19. *kept up tame*] confined, maintained, like a domesticated animal.

20. *Believe me!*] (This part-line could be linked, metrically, with either preceding or the following speech.)

22. *Utter*] (1) speak; (2) market, try to sell.

23. *Put . . . pipes*] i.e., Give it up. (See 1.3.256.)

24. *O' my faith*] On my faith. (An oath.)

26. *Sunday*] (Day when people are on their best behaviour, and likely to use particularly mild oaths.)

27. *evensong*] the service held at sunset.

28. *loose our handfast*] (1) let go of our firm grip; (2) fail to keep our sworn agreement (to resist the men). Ironic, since *handfast* could also mean 'betrothal'.

30. *Sinon*] Greek who persuaded the Trojans to accept the wooden horse (thus opening their gates to enemy invasion).

31. *wooden jade*] A 'jade' is an old female horse or an unruly woman, here applied to the Trojan horse and, metaphorically, to Petruccio; 'wooden' also means dull-witted or generally inferior.

Petruccio stole upon us? No, good sister.
Go home and tell the merry Greeks that sent you
Ilium shall burn, and I, as did Aeneas,
Will on my back, spite of the Myrmidons,   35
Carry this warlike lady, and, through seas
Unknown and unbelieved, seek out a land
Where, like a race of noble Amazons,
We'll root ourselves, and to our endless glory
Live, and despise base men.

Livia.   I'll second ye.   40

Bianca. How long have you been thus?

Livia.   That's all one, cousin;
I stand for freedom now.

Bianca.   Take heed of lying,
For, by this light, if we do credit you
And find you tripping, his infliction
That killed the Prince of Orange will be sport   45
To what we purpose.

Livia.   Let me feel the heaviest.

Maria. Swear by thy sweetheart Roland – for by your
      maidenhead
I fear 'twill be too late to swear – you mean
Nothing but fair and safe and honourable

---

33. *merry Greeks*] rowdy wantons. (Proverbial.)

34–40.] See Virgil's *Aeneid* Book II: after Sinon's betrayal, Aeneas carried his father on his back, out of burning Troy, and sailed west to found Rome.

34. *Ilium*] Trojan fortress-palace.

36. *this warlike lady*] Maria.

38. *Amazons*] warriors of the legendary all-female kingdom of Amazonia, which according to sixteenth-century report was located in South America (across seas 'unknown' to ancient Trojans and Romans).

41. *all one*] all the same.

44. *tripping*] making false steps.

44–5. *his . . . Orange*] The assassin of the Prince of Orange (leader of the Dutch rebellion against Spain) was dismembered and disembowelled alive, before having his heart torn out, his head chopped off, and his body quartered (1584). This was the standard punishment for treason in the period.

46. *To*] compared with.

Let . . . heaviest] Let me know the most solemn oath you can impose on me.

47–8. *by . . . swear*] i.e., I'm afraid you have no virginity left to swear upon.

To us and to our cause.
Livia.   I swear.
Bianca.   Stay yet.   50
　　Swear as you hate Moroso – that's the surest –
　　And as you have a Christian fear to find him
　　Worse than a poor dried jack, full of more aches
　　Than autumn has, more knavery and usury
　　And foolery and brokery than Dog's Ditch;   55
　　As you do constantly believe he's nothing
　　But an old empty bag with a grey beard,
　　And that beard such a bobtail that it looks
　　Worse than a mare's tail eaten off with fillies;
　　As you acknowledge that young handsome wench   60
　　That lies by such a bilbo-blade, that bends
　　With every pass he makes to th' hilts, most miserable,
　　A dry-nurse to his coughs, a fewterer
　　To such a nasty fellow, a robbed thing
　　Of all delights youth looks for, and (to end)   65
　　One cast away on coarse beef, born to brush
　　That everlasting cassock that has worn
　　As many servants out as the north-east passage
　　Has consumed sailors. If ye swear this, and truly,
　　Without the reservation of a gown   70

---

51. *surest*] surest oath.

53. *poor dried jack*] cheap, dried fish eaten by lower classes.

55. *brokery*] second-hand or inferior merchandise; underhanded dealings.
Dog's Ditch] Contemptuous term for Houndsditch, London, originally the ditch or moat outside the city wall, a receptacle for dead dogs and rubbish; later, a gathering site for sellers of old cloth.

59.] (Colts will eat the tails of mature horses with which they are pastured.)

61. *bilbo-blade*] (1) sword known for its elasticity and temper (from Bilboa, a town in Spain which forged such weapons); (2) Moroso's penis, which will 'bend . . . to the hilts' every time he makes a (sexual) 'pass'.

63. *dry nurse*] nursery attendant, 'dry' in contradistinction to the wet nurse whose job was to breastfeed infants (here, the dryness is also sexual).
fewterer] keeper of hounds.

66. *cast away on*] lost to a life of.

67. *cassock*] long coat.

68. *north-east passage*] (English and Dutch ships unsuccessfully searched for a north-east route to the Far East from 1553 to 1609.)

70. *reservation*] holding back.

> Or any meritorious petticoat,
> 'Tis like we shall believe you.

Livia.   I do swear it.

Maria. Stay yet a little. Came this wholesome motion –
> Deal truly, sister – from your own opinion,
> Or some suggestion of the foe?

Livia.   Ne'er fear me,   75
> For, by that little faith I have in husbands
> And the great zeal I bear your cause, I come
> Full of that liberty you stand for, sister.

Maria. If we believe, and you prove recreant, Livia,
> Think what a maim you give the noble cause   80
> We now stand up for. Think what women shall,
> A hundred year hence, speak thee, when examples
> Are looked for, and so great ones, whose relations,
> Spoke as we do 'em, wench, shall make new customs.

Bianca. If ye be false, repent, go home, and pray,   85
> And to the serious women of the city
> Confess yourself. Bring not a sin so heinous
> To load thy soul to this place. Mark me, Livia.
> If thou be'st double and betray'st our honours,
> And we fall in our purpose, get thee where   90
> There is no women living, nor no hope
> There ever shall be.

Maria.   If a mother's daughter
> That ever heard the name of stubborn husband
> Find thee and know thy sin –

Bianca.   Nay, if old age,
> One that has worn away the name of woman   95
> And no more left to know her by but railing,
> No teeth nor eyes, no legs but wooden ones,

---

72. *like*] likely.

79. *recreant*] deserter, traitor.

82. *speak*] speak of.

83. *relations*] stories.

84. *customs*] established usages which by long continuance have the force of law; taxes or tributes with this legal status.

86. *serious*] pious.

89. *double*] duplicitous.

90. *fall*] fail, are defeated.

Come but o'th' windward of thee – for sure she'll smell
   thee,
Thou'lt be so rank – she'll ride thee like a nightmare
And say her prayers backward to undo thee;   100
She'll curse thy meat and drink and, when thou marriest,
Clap a sound spell for ever on thy pleasures.

Maria. Children of five year old, like little fairies,
   Will pinch thee into motley; all that ever
   Shall live and hear of thee, I mean all women,   105
   Will, like so many Furies, shake their keys
   And toss their flaming distaffs o'er their heads,
   Crying 'revenge!' Take heed. 'Tis hideous.
   Oh, 'tis a fearful office! If thou hadst –
   Though thou be'st perfect now – when thou cam'st first   110
   A false imagination, get thee gone
   And, as my learnèd cousin said, repent.
   This place is sought by soundness.

Livia.   So I seek it,
   Or let me be a most despised example.

Maria. I do believe thee. Be thou worthy of it.   115
   You come not empty?

Livia.   No, here's cakes and cold meat
   And tripe of proof. Behold, here's wine and beer.

---

98. *o'th' windward*] downwind.

99. *nightmare*] female spirit supposed to settle on people at night, producing a feeling of suffocation.

100. *say . . . backwards*] (Witches were believed to cast spells by saying prayers backwards.)

102.] i.e., curse your sex-life.

104. *into motley*] i.e., into so many bruises that your skin will resemble the multicoloured clothing worn by fools.

106. *Furies*] Greek goddesses of vengeance, normally associated with torches and snakes.

keys] household keys, emblematic of their domestic duties.

107. *distaffs*] cleft staffs used in spinning (another female chore).

109. *office*] service, duty.

111. *false imagination*] secret thought.

113. *soundness*] constancy.

116. *empty*] empty-handed.

117. *tripe*] entrails of a cow or swine.

proof] high quality.

Be sudden; I shall be surprised else.
Maria.   Meet
    At the low parlour door; there lies a close way.
    What fond obedience ye have living in you   120
    Or duty to a man, before you enter
    Fling it away; 'twill but defile our off'rings.
Bianca. Be wary as you come.
Livia.   I warrant ye.
                  Exeunt [LIVIA *below, the others above*].

2.2

                  Enter ROLAND *at one door,* TRANIO *at the other.*

Tranio. Now, Roland!
Roland.   How do you?
Tranio.   How dost thou, man?
    Thou look'st ill.
Roland.   Yes. Pray, can you tell me, Tranio,
    Who knew the devil first?
Tranio.   A woman.
Roland.   So.
    Were they not well acquainted?
Tranio.   May be so,
    For they had certain dialogues together.   5
Roland. He sold her fruit, I take it?
Tranio.   Yes, and cheese
    That choked all mankind after.
Roland.   Canst thou tell me
    Whether that woman ever had a faith,
    After she had eaten?
Tranio.   That's a great school question.

---

    118. *surprised else*] caught otherwise.
    119. *close way*] secret passage.
    120. *What fond*] Whatever foolishly over-affectionate.

    2.2] Petronius's house.
    6. *fruit*] i.e., the fruit which Satan tempted Eve to eat.
    cheese] Eaten at the end of a meal, with fruit, and because of its texture
liable to cause choking (as at *Merry Wives*, 5.5.147, 'choked with a piece of
toasted cheese').
    9. *school question*] question debated by schoolmen (philosophers).

Roland. No, 'tis no question, for believe me, Tranio,   10
　　　That cold fruit, after eating, bred nought in her
　　　But windy promises and colic vows
　　　That broke out both ways. Thou hast heard, I am sure,
　　　Of Aesculapius, a far-famed surgeon,
　　　One that could set together quartered traitors   15
　　　And make 'em honest men.
Tranio.   How dost thou, Roland?
Roland. Let him but take (if he dare do a cure
　　　Shall get him fame indeed) a faithless woman
　　　(There will be credit for him; that will speak him),
　　　A broken woman, Tranio, a base woman,   20
　　　And, if he can cure such a wreck of honour,
　　　Let him come here and practise.
Tranio.   Now, for heaven's sake,
　　　What ail'st thou, Roland?
Roland.   I am ridden, Tranio,
　　　And spur-galled to the life of patience –
　　　Heaven keep my wits together! – by a thing   25
　　　Our worst thoughts are too noble for, a woman.
Tranio. Your mistress has a little frowned, it may be?
Roland. She *was* my mistress.
Tranio.   Is she not?
Roland.   No, Tranio.
　　　She has done me such disgrace, so spitefully,
　　　So like a woman bent to my undoing,   30
　　　That henceforth a good horse shall be my mistress,
　　　A good sword, or a book. And if you see her,

---

10. *'tis no question*] it's a certainty.
12. *colic*] of or pertaining to colic, the intestinal disturbance.
13. *both ways*] i.e., in flatulence and belching.
14. *Aesculapius*] Greek god of medicine.
15. *quartered*] drawn and quartered.
16. *How dost thou*] i.e., What do you mean?
18. *Shall*] that will.
19. *speak*] proclaim.
20. *broken*] faithless, a breaker of vows (also with the suggestion of the broken hymen).
21. *wreck*] (Punning on *rack* = 'cloud' and 'instrument of torture'.)
24. *spur-galled*] chaffed by a rider's spurs.
life] i.e., absolute limit.

Tell her, I do beseech you, even for love's sake,
Our old love and our friendship –
Tranio.   I will, Roland.
Roland. She may sooner count the good I have thought her,   35
Shed one true tear, mean one hour constantly,
Be old and honest, married and a maid,
Than make me see her more, or more believe her.
And, now I have met a messenger, farewell, sir.   *Exit.*
Tranio. Alas, poor Roland! I will do it for thee.   40
This is that dog Moroso. But I hope
To see him cold i'th' mouth ere he enjoy her.
I'll watch this young man. Desperate thoughts may
   seize him,
And, if my purse or counsel can, I'll ease him.   *Exit.*

2.3

Enter PETRUCCIO, PETRONIUS, SOPHOCLES, *and* MOROSO.

Petruccio. For look you, gentlemen, say that I grant her,
Out of my free and liberal love, a pardon,
Which you and all men else know she deserves not –
Teneatis, amici – can all the world leave laughing?
Petronius. I think not.
Petruccio.   No, by this hand, they cannot.   5
For, pray, consider: have you ever read,
Or heard of, or can any man imagine,
So stiff a tomboy, of so set a malice
And such a brazen resolution

---

35. *count*] reckon up.
36. *mean . . . constantly*] be faithful one hour.
37. *honest*] chaste.
39. *a messenger*] i.e., you.
42. *cold i'th' mouth*] i.e., defeated or possibly dead. (Said of hunting dogs that have lost the scent.)

2.3] Petronius's house.
4. Teneatis, amici] 'Grasp this, friends': a rhetorical catch-phrase.
leave] stop.
8. *stiff*] stubborn.
tomboy] unruly or immodest woman.

As this young crab-tree? And then answer me –   10
And mark but this too, friends: without a cause,
Not a foul word come 'cross her, not a fear
She justly can take hold on – and do you think
I must sleep out my anger and endure it,
Sew pillows to her ease and lull her mischief?   15
Give me a spindle first! No, no, my masters,
Were she as fair as Nell o' Greece, and housewife
As good as the wise sailor's wife, and young still,
Never above fifteen, and these tricks to it,
She should ride the wild mare once a week, she should,   20
Believe me, friends, she should. I would tabor her
Till all the legions that are crept into her
Flew out with fire i'th' tails.
Sophocles.   Methinks you err now,
And to me seems a little sufferance
Were a far surer cure.
Petruccio.   Yes, I can suffer,   25
Where I see promises of peace and 'mendment.
Moroso. Give her a few conditions.
Petruccio.   I'll be hanged first.
Petronius. Give her a crab-tree cudgel.
Petruccio.   So I will,
And after it a flock-bed for her bones,
And hard eggs, till they brace her like a drum.   30

---

10. *crab-tree*] (Crab-apple trees are crooked, and their fruit sour.)

16. *Give . . . spindle*] Turn me into a woman (by making me take up the demeaning female task of sewing).

17. *Nell o' Greece*] Helen of Troy.

18. *wise sailor's*] Ulysses's wife Penelope was famous for her fidelity and housekeeping.

20. *ride . . . mare*] be punished by being forced to sit on an uncomfortable wooden frame. (With sexual innuendo.)

21. *tabor*] beat on. (A tabor is a drum.)

22–3. *Till . . . tails*] until the legions of devils that have crept into her flew out with fire in their tails. (Devils were sometimes depicted with flaming posteriors.)

24. *seems*] it seems that.

sufferance] patience, forbearance.

29. *flock-bed*] bed stuffed with flock, a coarse material, and hence uncomfortable (especially for someone bedridden as a result of a severe beating).

bones] (broken) bones.

30. *hard eggs*] hard-boiled eggs, considered constipating.

She shall be pampered with [a shit-hole stopper].
She shall not know a stool in ten months, gentlemen.
Sophocles. This must not be.

Enter JAQUES.

Jaques.   Arm, arm, out with your weapons!
For all the women in the kingdom's on ye.
They swarm like wasps, and nothing can destroy 'em   35
But stopping of their hive and smothering of 'em.

Enter PEDRO.

Pedro. Stand to your guard, sir! All the devils extant
Are broke upon us like a cloud of thunder.
There are more women marching hitherward,
In rescue of my mistress, than e'er turned tail   40
At Sturbridge Fair – and, I believe, as fiery.
Jaques. The forlorn hope's led by a tanner's wife
(I know her by her hide), a desperate woman.
She flayed her husband in her youth, and made
Reins of his hide to ride the parish; her placket   45
Looks like the straits of Gibraltar, still wider
Down to the gulf; all sunburnt Barbary

---

31. *pampered*] overfed, fed delicacies.
a shit-hole stopper] (1) food that will make her constipated; (2) something inserted into her rectum (like a tobacco pipe stopper, bottle-plug, or penis).
32. *know a stool*] move her bowels.
ten months] (Conventional term of a pregnancy.)
33. *weapons*] (Suggesting penises.)
37. *devils*] (Misogynists often compared women to devils; the metaphor is continued in *tail* and *fiery*.)
40. *turned tail*] (1) ran away; (2) danced in circles; (3) turned tricks, offered themselves for sexual penetration.
41. *Sturbridge Fair*] annual market fair near Cambridge.
42. *forlorn hope's*] picked body of troops leading a dangerous military attack is.
44. *flayed her husband*] See introduction p. 19.
45. *placket*] slit at the top of a skirt or petticoat, allowing its removal; often used as a euphemism for a woman's genitals.
47. *gulf*] (1) area of ocean partially enclosed by land; (2) deep abyss, devouring whirlpool; (3) vagina.
sunburnt] dark-skinned.
Barbary] North Africa.

Lies in her breech. Take 'em all together,
They are a genealogy of jennets, gotten
And born thus by the boisterous breath of husbands.   50
They serve sure, and are swift to catch occasion
(I mean, their foes or husbands) by the forelock,
And there they hang like favours. Cry they can,
But more for noble spite than fear, and crying,
Like the old giants that were foes to heaven,   55
They heave ye stool on stool, and fling main pot-lids
Like massy rocks, dart ladles, toasting irons
And tongs like thunderbolts till, overlaid,
They fall beneath the weight – yet still aspiring
At those imperious codsheads that would tame 'em.   60
There's ne'er a one of these, the worst and weakest –
Choose where you will – but dare attempt the raising,
Against the sovereign peace of Puritans,
A maypole or a morris, maugre mainly

---

48. *breech*] (1) butt; (2) breeches, pants.

49. *genealogy . . . gotten*] race or species of small Spanish horses, allegedly impregnated by the west wind (thus accounting for their speed), begotten or acquired.

50. *born*] (1) given birth; (2) endured, borne.

breath] (This combines an allusion to Genesis 2:7, where God breathes life into Adam, with the legend of Spanish mares impregnated by the wind.)

51. *sure*] reliably.

51–2. *catch . . . forelock*] 'Occasion' or opportunity was often personified as a semi-bald woman with a long forelock one might grab when she approached, but could not grab after she passed.

52. *forelock*] (Playing on the sense 'part of a horse's harness'.)

53. *favours*] tokens of affection (like ribbons, tied in the hair).

55. *old . . . heaven*] race of giants who, in Greek mythology, rebelled against the gods and were punished by confinement in the earth, where they became volcanoes such as Mount Etna.

56. *main*] heavy, big.

57. *dart ladles*] throw ladles like spears.

toasting irons] metal prongs used for toasting food over an open fire.

60. *codsheads*] (1) godheads (continuing the allusion to the giants of Greek mythology); (2) husbands as 'heads' of households, and as God's substitutes within a family; (3) bone-heads ('codshead' was an insult playing on 'fish-heads' and on 'cod' as testicle).

63–4. *Against . . . morris*] (Puritans were opposed to dances like the maypole and the morris.)

64. *maugre*] despite.

Their zeals and dudgeon daggers – and yet more,   65
Dares plant a stand of battering ale against 'em
And drink 'em out o'th' parish.
Pedro. There's one first brought in the bears, against the
    canons
Of two churchwardens, made it good, and fought 'em –
And in the churchyard, after evensong.   70
Jaques. Another, to her everlasting fame, erected
Two ale-houses of ease, the quarter sessions
Running against her roundly; in which business
Two of the disannullers lost their night-caps,
A third stood excommunicate by the cudgel.   75
The cuntstable, to her eternal glory,
Drunk hard and was converted, and she victor.
Sophocles. Lo ye, fierce Petruccio,
This comes of your impatience.
Petruccio.   Come, to council!
Sophocles. Now ye must grant conditions, or the kingdom   80
Will have no other talk but this.
Petronius.   Away then,
And let's advise the best.
Sophocles. [*To Moroso*]   Why do you tremble?
Moroso. Have I lived thus long to be knocked o'th' head

---

65. *dudgeon daggers*] daggers made of inferior materials.
66. *plant . . . ale*] (Likening ale bottles to weapons which would be used
in a military stand against one's enemies – here, Puritans, opposed to drinking alcohol.)
68. *brought . . . bears*] (Referring to the animal-baiting games which were
a popular sport and pastime – but very inappropriate on church property.)
canons] regulations (also punning on 'cannons').
69. *made it good*] justified their behaviour.
fought 'em] (1) battled with the churchwardens; (2) had the bears fight
with dogs.
72. *ale-houses of ease*] (1) taverns; (2) brothels.
quarter sessions] court sessions held four times a year.
73. *Running . . . roundly*] i.e., going badly for her.
74. *disannullers*] persons who deprive another of his or her title.
75. *excommunicate*] i.e., evicted.
76–7.] i.e., She got the constable drunk and won him over, to the eternal
glory of the proprietress of the alehouse or brothel. (The bawdy pun on
'cunt-stable' suggests he was plied with more than ale.)

With half a washing-beetle?–Pray, be wise, sir.
Petruccio. Come. Something I'll do, but what it is, I know not.   85
Sophocles. To council then, and let's avoid these follies.
Guard all the doors, or we shall not have a cloak left.

Exeunt.

2.4

Enter three Country Wenches *at several doors.*

First. How goes your business, girls?
Second.   Afoot and fair.
Third. If fortune favour us. Away to your strengths!
     We are discovered else.
First. The country forces are arrived. Begone!
Second. Arm, and be valiant! Think of our cause!   5
Third. Our justice!
First.   Ay, ay, 'tis sufficient.   *Exeunt.*

2.5

Enter PETRONIUS, PETRUCCIO, MOROSO, SOPHOCLES,
and TRANIO.

Petronius. I am indifferent – though, I must confess,
     I had rather see her carted.
Tranio.   No more of that, sir.
Sophocles. [*To Petruccio*] Are ye resolved to give her fair
          conditions?

---

84. *washing-beetle*] a wooden bat used to beat or pound clothes during washing.

85. *Something ... not*] (A parody of Shakespeare's *History of King Lear* 2.2.454–5: 'I will do such things – / What they are, yet I know not'.)

86. *avoid*] defeat; quash.

2.4] Near Petronius's house.
1. *Afoot*] i.e., Moving along.
2. *strengths*] strongholds.

2.5] Petronius's house.
2. *carted*] carted to jail, as was done to prostitutes and other recreant women. (The cart exposed its unhappy passengers to public humiliation.)

'Twill be the safest way.

Petruccio.   I am distracted.
Would I had run my head into a halter   5
When I first wooed her! If I offer peace,
She'll urge her own conditions: there's the devil.

Sophocles. Why, say she do?

Petruccio.   Say I am made an ass, then!
I know her aim. May I with reputation –
Answer me this – with safety of mine honour,   10
After the mighty manage of my first wife,
Which was indeed a Fury to this filly,
After my twelve strong labours to reclaim her,
Which would have made Don Hercules horn-mad
And hid him in his hide, suffer this Cicely,   15
Ere she have warmed my sheets, ere grappled with me,
This pink, this painted foist, this cockle-boat,
To hang her fights out and defy me, friends,
A well-known man-of-war? If this be equal

---

5. *halter*] (1) head-gear used to steer horses; (2) noose.

7. *the devil*] what bedevils me.

8. *say*] suppose.

11. *manage*] training (playing on the sense 'manège', specifically training a horse).

12. *to*] compared with.

13–15. *twelve . . . hide*] (Petruccio plays on the legend of 'Don' [Sir] Hercules and the twelve labours that included tearing the hide from the Nemean lion.)

14. *horn-mad*] mad as a horned animal. (Also alluding to the cuckold's horns.)

15. *Cicely*] name associated with lower-class women or servants, as in *The Taming of the Shrew*, 'Cicely Hackett. / . . . The woman's maid' (In. 2.88–9) and *Two Noble Kinsmen*, 'Cicely, the sempster's daughter' (3.5.45).

16. *grappled*] struggled physically in a sexual sense. (Also anticipating the ensuing metaphor of naval warfare: a grapple is a hooked implement used to pull down fortifications or draw one man-of-war alongside another.)

17. *pink*] (1) small fishing boat; (2) whore.
painted] (Alluding to cosmetics.)
foist] (1) a light sailing vessel; (2) a rogue, cheat; (3) a silent fart.
cockle-boat] another small boat. (But continuing the sexual innuendo with 'cock'.)

18. *fights*] screens used during a naval engagement to conceal and protect the crew of the vessel.

19. *man-of-war*] heavy battleship.
equal] even-handed; just.

And I may suffer, say, and I have done.   20
Petronius. I do not think you may.
Tranio.   You'll make it worse, sir.
Sophocles. Pray, hear me, good Petruccio. But even now
    You were contented to give all conditions,
    To try how far she would carry. 'Tis a folly –
    And you will find it so – to clap the curb on   25
    Ere ye be sure it proves a natural wildness
    And not a forced. Give her conditions,
    For, on my life, this trick is put into her –
Petronius. I should believe so too.
Sophocles. [*To Petruccio*]   And not her own.
Tranio. [*To Petruccio*] You'll find it so.
Sophocles. [*To Petruccio*]   Then, if she founder with you,   30
    Clap spurs on, and in this you'll deal with temperance,
    Avoid the hurry of the world –

                                        Music above.
Tranio. [*To Petruccio*]   and lose –
Moroso. [*To Petruccio*] No honour, o' my life, sir.
Petruccio.   I will do it.
Petronius. It seems they are very merry.
Petruccio.   Why, God hold it!

                Enter JAQUES.

Moroso. Now, Jaques!
Jaques.   They are i'th' flaunt, sir.
Sophocles.   Yes, we hear 'em.   35
Jaques. They have got a stick of fiddles, and they firk it
    In wondrous ways. The two grand capitanos

---

20. *say*] say so.
have done] i.e., give it up, having said my say.
24. *carry*] (as a horse its rider).
25. *curb*] a chain or strap attached to a horse's bit.
28. *this trick . . . her*] i.e., she was put up to this trick.
29. *own*] own idea.
30. *founder*] stumble, fall violently (said of horses).
34. *hold*] continue.
35. *i'th' flaunt*] i.e., flaunting themselves.
36. *stick of fiddles*] (1) fiddle-stick; (2) penis or dildo.
firk] (1) jig, dance; (2) fuck.
37. *capitanos*] captains.

That brought the auxiliary regiments
Dance with their coats tucked up to their bare breeches
And bid the kingdom kiss 'em; that's the burden.   40
They have got metheglin and audacious ale
And talk like tyrants.

Petronius.   How know'st thou?

Jaques.   I peeped in
At a loose latchet.

Tranio.   Hark!

Petronius.   A song. Pray, silence.

Women. [*Within, singing*]
A health, for all this day,
To the woman that bears the sway,   45
    And wears the breeches.
        Let it come, let it come!
Let this health be a seal
For the good of the commonweal
    The woman shall wear the breeches.   50
Let's drink then, and laugh it,
And merrily, merrily quaff it,
And tipple and tipple a round.
    Here's to thy fool
    And to my fool!   55
        Come, to all fools!
Though it cost us, wench, many a pound.

Enter above MARIA, BIANCA, *a* City Wife, *a* Country Wife,
        and three [Country Wenches].

Moroso. [*To the men*] They look out.
Petruccio. Good even, ladies!
Maria.   [God] you good even, sir!

---

39. *coats*] skirts.
40. *burden*] (1) chorus, refrain; (2) sexual partner.
41. *metheglin*] spiced mead.
43. *latchet*] latch. (A loose inner door-latch would enable one to force the door open a crack from outside.)
49. *commonweal*] commonwealth; republic (suggesting that male sovereignty has been replaced with a more egalitarian form of government).
52. *quaff*] guzzle.
53. *tipple*] drink.
59. *God . . . even*] God give you a good evening.

Petruccio. How have you slept tonight?
Maria.   Exceeding well, sir.   60
Petruccio. Did you not wish me with you?
Maria.   No, believe me,
    I never thought upon you.
Country Wife. [*To Bianca*]   Is that he?
Bianca.   Yes.
Country Wife. [*To Petruccio*] Sir!
Sophocles. [*To the men*] She has drunk hard: mark her hood.
Country Wife. [*To Petruccio*]   You are –
Sophocles. [*To the men*] Learnèdly drunk, I'll hang else. Let
    her utter.
Country Wife. [*To Petruccio*] And I must tell you, *viva voce*,
    friend,   65
    A very foolish fellow.
Tranio. [*To the men*]   There's an ale figure.
Petruccio. [*To Country Wife*] I thank you, Susan Brotes.
City Wife. [*To Country Wife*]   Forward, sister.
Country Wife. You have espousèd here a hearty woman,
    A comely, and courageous.
Petruccio.   Well, I have so.
Country Wife. And – to the comfort of distressèd damsels,   70
    Women outworn in wedlock, and such vessels –
    This woman has defied you.
Petruccio.   It should seem so.
Country Wife. And why?
Petruccio.   Yes, can you tell?
Country Wife.   For thirteen causes.

---

63. *mark*] (1) notice; (2) heed, consider.

hood] (1) woman's cap; (2) garment worn by churchmen and academics, still used in graduations to honour the doctoral degree. Here sarcastic: women were barred from the universities and the pulpit.

65. viva voce] with live voice; loudly.

66. *ale figure*] rhetorical figure of speech inspired by drunkenness.

67. *Susan Brotes*] (Presumably a satirical allusion to a mythical martial woman, but its referent has never been identified.)

67, 74, 87. *sister*] fellow Christian. (An idiom associated with Puritans.)

71. *vessels*] (Alluding to the notion of the female body as a 'weaker vessel', frailer container for the soul – but in context also suggesting 'container for liquor'.)

Petruccio. Pray, by your patience, mistress –
City Wife. [*To Country Wife*]   Forward, sister.
Petruccio. [*To Country Wife*] Do you mean to treat of all these?
City Wife.   Who shall let her?   75
Petronius. Do you hear, velvet-hood? We come not now
    To hear your doctrine.
Country Wife.   For the first, I take it,
    It doth divide itself in seven branches.
Petruccio. Hark you, good Maria:
    Have you got a catechizer here?
Tranio. [*To Country Wife*]   Good zeal!   80
Sophocles. [*To Country Wife*] Good three-piled predication,
    will you peace
    And hear the cause we come for?
Country Wife.   Yes, bobtails,
    We know the cause you came for. Here's the cause.
    But never hope to carry her, never dream
    Or flatter your opinions with a thought   85
    Of base repentance in her.
City Wife.   Give me sack.
                          [*One gives her sack.*]
    By this, and next, strong ale –
Country Wife.   Swear forward, sister.
City Wife. By all that's cordial, in this place we'll bury

---

74. *Pray . . . mistress*] (Petruccio asks to be listened to in exaggeratedly polite speech.)

75. *treat of*] negotiate.
let] hinder.

77. *For the first*] As for the first cause.

80. *catechizer*] teacher of catechism or Church doctrine.
zeal] associated with Puritans.

81. *three-piled*] (Three-piled velvet is thicker and costlier.)
predication] a loud proclamation.
peace] be quiet.

82. *bobtails*] i.e., rascals.

83. *the cause*] i.e., Maria.

84. *carry her*] (1) carry her away, as in triumph; (2) carry her sexually.

86. *sack*] a sweet white wine.

87. *By this*] (She swears by the sack.)
Swear forward] Go ahead and swear.

88. *cordial*] Punning on sense of 'comforting, good for the heart' and the alcoholic beverage.

Our bones, fames, tongues, our triumphs, and ev'n all
That ever yet was chronicled of woman, 90
But this brave wench, this excellent despiser,
This bane of dull obedience, shall inherit
Her liberal will, and march off with conditions
Noble and worth herself.

Country Wife. [*To the men*]　　She shall, Tom Tylers –
And brave ones too. My hood shall make a hearse-cloth, 95
And I lie under it like Joan o' Gaunt,
Ere I go less; my distaff stuck up by me,
For the eternal trophy of my conquests,
And loud Fame at my head with two main bottles
Shall fill to all the world the glorious fall 100
Of old Dame Gillian.

City Wife. [*To the men*]　　Yet a little further.
We have taken arms in rescue of this lady,
Most just and noble. If ye beat us off,
Without conditions, and we recreant,

---

89. *fames*] reputations.

90. *chronicled*] recorded in history books.

91. *But*] unless.

92. *inherit*] obtain.

93. *Her liberal will*] all her desires.

94. *Tom Tylers*] (Referring to the wimpy protagonist of another shrew-taming play, the anonymous *Tom Tyler and His Wife* (1560). Tyler's violently shrewish wife, aptly named Strife, remains untamed despite a brutal beating administered by his friend.)

95. *hearse-cloth*] funeral pall.

96. *Joan o' Gaunt*] Punning on John of Gaunt, fourteenth-century prince who was popularly believed to have conquered Portugal.

97. *Ere . . . less*] before I settle for less.

99. *main*] great.

100. *fill to*] i.e., raise a glass to, toast.

101. *Gillian*] another woman's name with lower-class associations.

101–9.] The passage parodies the ceremony for stripping a man of his knighthood: hewing off the spurs, tearing off the coat of arms, breaking the sword.

102. *taken*] taken up.

103. *beat us off*] defeat us. (Possibly with a sexual innuendo.)

104. *be recreant*] i.e., give up our cause.

Use us as we deserve, and first degrade us   105
Of all our ancient chambering; next that,
The symbols of our secrecy, silk stockings,
Hew off our heels; our petticoats of arms
Tear off our bod'ces, and our bodkins break
Over our coward heads.

Country Wife. [*To the men*]   And ever after,   110
To make the tainture most notorious,
At all our crests (*videlicet*, our plackets)
Let laces hang, and we return again
Into our former titles, dairy maids.

Petruccio. No more wars! Puissant ladies, show conditions,   115
And freely I accept 'em.

Maria. [*To the women*]   Call in Livia.
She's in the treaty too.

Moroso.   How, Livia?

Enter LIVIA *above.*

Maria.   Heard you that, sir?–
[*She throws a paper down.*]
There's the conditions for you; pray, peruse 'em.
[*Petruccio reads the paper silently.*]

Petronius. [*To Moroso*] Yes, there she is. 'T had been no right
rebellion,

105–6. *degrade . . . chambering*] strip us of (1) our age-old privilege to
behave lasciviously ('chambering' can denote activities in the bed-chamber);
(2) our privilege to be lustful at an advanced age. The phrase 'ancient chambering' also fleetingly suggests the chamber in which a lord or dignitary
would conduct his affairs of state.

petticoats of arms] (A pun on 'coats of arms'; a petticoat is a female
undergarment.)

109. *bod'ces*] bodices.

bodkins] (1) daggers; (2) hairpins.

110. *coward*] cowardly.

111. *tainture*] defilement, disgrace.

112. videlicet] that is to say.

plackets] slits at the tops of petticoats.

113. *Let laces hang*] i.e., let our petticoats hang open, suggesting both
slovenliness and sexual availability.

114. *dairy maids*] i.e., lower-class, 'rustic' types. (There may also be a joke
in the illogic of 'return again / Into . . . maids'.)

115. *Puissant*] Powerful.

119. *right*] true.

Had she held off. What think you, man?

Moroso.   Nay, nothing.   120
  I have enough o'th' prospect. O' my conscience,
  The world's end and the goodness of a woman
  Will come together.

Petronius. [*To Livia*]   Are you there, sweet lady?

Livia. Cry you mercy, sir. I saw you not. [*Kneeling*] Your
      blessing?

Petronius. Yes, when I bless a jade that stumbles with me.   125
[*To Petruccio*] How are the articles?

Livia. [*To Moroso*]   This is for you, sir.
                    [*She throws a paper down to Moroso.*]
  And I shall think upon't.

Moroso.   You have used me finely.

Livia. There is no other use of thee now extant
  But to be hung up, cassock, cap, and all,
  For some strange monster at apothecaries.   130

Petronius. I hear you, whore.

Livia.   It must be his, then, sir,
  For need will then compel me.

City Wife.   Blessing on thee!

Petronius. There's no talking to 'em. – How are they, sir?

Petruccio. As I expected: [*Reading*] liberty and clothes,
  When and in what way she will; continual moneys,   135
  Company, and all the house at her dispose;
  No tongue to say 'Why is this?' or 'Whither will it?'
  New coaches, and some buildings, she appoints here,

122–3. *The world's . . . together*] i.e., No good woman will ever be found.
130. *For*] as.

strange . . . apothecaries] (Druggists sometimes displayed preserved marvellous or exotic creatures.)

131–2. *It . . . me*] i.e., I would then be Moroso's whore. (Livia rebuts her father's insult by defining a forced marriage as a kind of whoredom, either in itself as her being 'sold' by her father, or because sexual dissatisfaction will drive her to unchastity.)

133. *they*] the articles.

135. *will*] wills; will have it.

136. *dispose*] disposal.

137. *Whither will it?*] Where are you going? (With condescension suggested by 'it', normally used of children.)

138. *appoints*] stipulates.

Hangings and hunting horses, and for plate
And jewels for her private use, I take it,   140
Two thousand pounds in present; then for music
And women to read French –
Petronius.   This must not be.
Petruccio. And at the latter end a clause put in
That Livia shall by no man be importuned,
This whole month yet, to marry.
Petronius.   This is monstrous!   145
Petruccio. This shall be done. I'll humour her a while.
If nothing but repentance and undoing
Can win her love, I'll make a shift for one.
Sophocles. [*Aside to Petruccio*] When ye are once a-bed, all
    these conditions
Lie under your own seal.
Maria. [*To Petruccio*]   Do ye like 'em?
Petruccio.   Yes.   150
And, by that faith I gave ye fore the priest,
I'll ratify 'em.
Country Wife. Stay! What pledges?
Maria. No, I'll take that oath –
But have a care ye keep it.
City Wife. [*To Petruccio*]   ''Tis not now   155
As when Andrea lived.'
Country Wife. [*To Petruccio*] If ye do juggle,
Or alter but a letter of this creed
We have set down, the self-same persecution –

---

139. *Hangings*] tapestries, wall-hangings.

141. *Two thousand pounds*] (a huge sum of money, indicating that Petruccio has the income of an aristocrat or a very wealthy London merchant).

in present] immediately.

142. *read*] teach.

148. *make . . . one*] i.e., give it one try, for my part.

150. *seal*] (The male role in intercourse was seen as similar to the imprinting of a seal in wax; metaphorically, Petruccio can rewrite the terms of the settlement once the marriage is consummated and his conjugal authority instated.)

151. *faith*] i.e., the marriage oath.

155–6. ''Tis . . . lived.'] (Quoting Thomas Kyd's popular play *The Spanish Tragedy* 3.12.11, which became an expression of nostalgia.)

156. *juggle*] quibble.

Maria. Mistrust him not.
Petruccio.　　　　　　By all my honesty –
Maria. Enough. I yield.
Petronius. [*Reading the paper*] What's this inserted here?　　160
Sophocles. [*Reading*] 'That the two valiant women that
　　　command here
　　Shall have a supper made 'em, and a large one,
　　And liberal entertainment without grudging,
　　And pay for all their soldiers.'
Petruccio.　　　　　　That shall be too –
　　And, if a tun of wine will serve to pay 'em,　　165
　　They shall have justice. I ordain ye all
　　Paymasters, gentlemen.
Tranio. [*To the men*]　　Then we shall have sport, boys.
Maria. [*To the men*] We'll meet ye in the parlour.
　　　　　　　　　　[*Exeunt women above.*]
Petruccio. [*To Petronius*]　　　　Ne'er look sad, sir,
　　For I will do it.
Sophocles. [*To Petronius*] There's no danger in't.
Petruccio. [*To Petronius*] For Livia's article, you shall observe
　　it;　　170
　　I have tied myself.
Petronius.　　　　I will.
Petruccio.　　　　　　Along then! – Now
　　Either I break, or this stiff plant must bow.
　　　　　　　　　　Exeunt [*men below*].

---

162. *made 'em*] made for them.
163. *liberal*] generous.
165. *tun*] barrel.
167. *Paymasters*] in charge of payment.
170. *For*] As for.
171. *tied*] obligated.
172. *bow*] bend. (With a sexual joke on 'stiff'.)

Act 3

Enter ROLAND *and* TRANIO.

Tranio. Come, ye shall take my counsel.
Roland.   I shall hang first.
    I'll no more love, that's certain. 'Tis a bane,
    Next that they poison rats with, the most mortal.
    No, I thank heaven, I have got my sleep again,
    And now begin to write sense. I can walk ye   5
    A long hour in my chamber like a man,
    And think of something that may better me,
    Some serious point of learning or my state.
    No more 'Ay me!'s and *misereri*s, Tranio,
    Come near my brain. I'll tell thee: had the devil   10
    But any essence in him of a man
    And could be brought to love, and love a woman,
    'Twould make his head ache worser than his horns do,
    And firk him with a fire he never felt yet
    Would make him dance. I tell thee, there is nothing –   15
    It may be thy case, Tranio, therefore hear me –
    Under the sun (reckon the mass of follies
    Crept into th' world with man) so desperate,
    So mad, so senseless, poor and base, so wretched,

    3.1] Somewhere in London.

    2–3. *'Tis . . . mortal*] It is a poison almost as deadly as that with which they poison rats.

    5. *walk ye*] walk.

    8. *state*] state of affairs.

    9. misereris] pleas for mercy. (Referring to the musical setting of one of the penitential psalms.)

    11. *But any*] any.

    14. *firk*] goad.

    15. *Would*] that would.

Roguey and scurvy –

Tranio.   Whither wilt thou, Roland?   20

Roland. As 'tis to be in love.

Tranio.   And why, for [God's] sake?

Roland. And why, for [God's] sake? Dost thou not conceive
      me?

Tranio. No, by my troth.

Roland.   Pray, then, and heartily,
      For fear thou fall into't. I'll tell thee why too,
      For I have hope to save thee: when thou lov'st,   25
      And first begin'st to worship the gilt calf
      With the white face, *imprimis*, thou has lost thy gentry
      And, like a prentice, flung away thy freedom.
      Forthwith thou art a slave.

Tranio.   That's a new doctrine.

Roland. Next, thou art no more a man.

Tranio.   What, then?   30

Roland. A frippery.
      Nothing but braided hair and penny ribbon,
      Glove, garter, ring, rose – or, at best, a swabber.
      If thou canst love so near to keep thy making,

---

20. *Roguey*] rascally.

scurvy] a term of disapprobation, from scurvy, a disfiguring vitamin
deficiency.

Whither wilt thou?] i.e., What is your point?

22. *conceive*] comprehend.

26. *gilt calf*] (Alluding to the golden idol Moses chastised his people for
worshipping.)

27. *white face*] (Women wore white make-up; dark complexions were considered masculine.)

imprimis] in the first place. (The phrase generally introduces a list or
inventory in a will).

lost thy gentry] lost your status as gentleman; debased yourself.

29. *Forthwith*] Immediately.

30. *What, then?*] What do I become, then?

31. *frippery*] piece of tawdry dress.

33. *garter*] band which secures the hose or stockings, worn by men as well
as women.

rose] (decorative, on shoes or clothing).

swabber] mop for cleaning ovens.

34. *making*] true nature.

        Yet thou wilt lose thy language.
Tranio.   Why?
Roland.   Oh, Tranio,   35
        Those things in love ne'er talk as we do.
Tranio.   No?
Roland. No, without doubt. They sigh and shake the head
        And sometimes whistle dolefully.
Tranio.   No tongue?
Roland. Yes, Tranio, but no truth in't, nor no reason.
        And when they cant (for 'tis a kind of canting),   40
        Ye shall hear, if you reach to understand 'em
        (Which you must be a fool first, or you cannot),
        Such gibberish, such 'believe me, I protest, sweet',
        And 'O dear heavens, in which such constellations
        Reign at the births of lovers, this is too well',   45
        And 'deign me, lady, deign me, I beseech ye,
        Your poor unworthy lump' – and then she licks him.
Tranio. A pox on't, this is nothing.
Roland.   Thou hast hit it.
        Then talks she ten times worse, and wries and wriggles
        As though she had the itch – and so it may be.   50
Tranio. Of what religion are they?
Roland.   Good old Catholics.
        They deal by intercession all: they keep
        A kind of household gods, called chambermaids,
        Which, being prayed to, and their off'rings brought
        (Which are in gold; yet some observe the old law   55

---

    36. *things*] i.e., men.
    40. *cant*] speak in jargon.
    41. *reach*] try.
    46. *deign*] condescend to think.
    47. *licks*] (A mother bear was believed to lick her unformed cubs
['lumps'] into shape; Rowland suggests that men in love are like newborns,
whose identity is completely shaped by the woman. There may also be an
allusion to oral sex.)
    48. *A pox on't*] (An expression of contempt.)
    Thou . . . it] i.e., You've got it.
    49. *wries*] writhes.
    50. *itch*] skin disease (possibly venereal) producing inflammation and
pustules.
    52. *intercession*] (of the saints: a belief rejected by Protestantism)
    55. *old law*] Old Testament ritual.

And give 'em flesh), *probatum est*, you shall have
As good love for your money, and as tidy,
As e'er you turned your leg o'er; and, that ended –
Tranio. Why, thou art grown a strange discoverer.
Roland. Of mine own follies, Tranio.
Tranio.   Wilt thou, Roland,   60
Certain ne'er love again?
Roland.   [O' God's name], certain.
And if I be not dead drunk, I shall keep it.
Tranio. Tell me but this: what dost thou think of women?
Roland. Why, as I think of fiddles: they delight me
Till their strings break.
Tranio.   What strings?
Roland.   Their modesties,   65
Faiths, vows, and maidenheads – for they are like kits,
They have but four strings to 'em.
Tranio.   What wilt thou
Give me for ten pound now, when thou next lov'st,
And the same woman still?
Roland.   Give me the money.
A hundred, and my bond for't.
Tranio.   But, pray, hear me: 70
I'll work all means I can to reconcile ye.
Roland. Do, do. Give me the money.
Tranio. [*Giving money*]   There.
Roland.   Work, Tranio.

---

56. *flesh*] (1) blood sacrifice; (2) meat; (3) sex.
probatum est] it is proven.
57. *tidy*] worthy, excellent.
58. *turned . . . over*] mounted (as of a horse).
59. *discoverer*] informer; one who discloses a secret.
61. *Certain*] surely.
O' God's name] In the name of God. (A strong oath.)
62. *keep it*] i.e., keep this vow.
65. *modesties*] (The last syllable was pronounced 'ties', here punning on 'strings'.)
66. *kits*] small fiddles.
70. *bond*] promissory note. (Rowland bets ten to one that he will not love Livia again.)
71. *work all means*] i.e., try everything.

Tranio. You shall go sometimes where she is.
Roland.   Yes, straight.
    This is the first good I e'er got by woman.
Tranio. You would think it strange now, if another beauty   75
    As good as hers, say better –
Roland.   Well?
Tranio.   Conceive me,
    This is no point o'th' wager.
Roland.   That's all one.
Tranio. Love ye as much, or more, than she now hates ye.
Roland. 'Tis a good hearing. Let 'em love! Ten pound more
    I never love that woman.
Tranio. [*Giving money*]   There it is.   80
    And so a hundred, if ye lose.
Roland.   'Tis done.
    Have ye another to put in?
Tranio.   No more, sir.
Roland. I am very sorry. Now will I erect
    A new game, and go hate for th' bell. I am sure
    I am in excellent case to win.
Tranio.   I must have leave   85
    To tell ye, and tell truth too, what she is
    And how she suffers for you.
Roland.   Ten pound more
    I never believe ye.
Tranio.   No, sir, I am stinted.

---

73. *straight*] directly.
74. *This*] The bet Rowland thinks he will win.
75–80.] (Tranio gets Roland to bet another £10 that, if an unnamed woman more beautiful than Livia were to love him as strongly as Livia now hates him, he will not reciprocate her love.)
77. *This . . . wager*] What I'm about to say is not what we bet on.
all one] one and the same.
79. *hearing*] news, report.
82. *another . . . in*] i.e., another £10 to bet.
83–4. *erect . . . game*] start a new competition.
84. *hate*] hate women.
bell] prize.
85. *case*] position.
leave] permission.
88. *stinted*] finished (having run out of money).

Roland. Well, take your best way, then.
Tranio.   Let's walk. I am glad
     Your sullen fever's off.
Roland.   Shalt see me, Tranio,   90
     A monstrous merry man now. Let's to the wedding.
     And as we go, tell me the general hurry
     Of these mad wenches and their works.
Tranio.   I will.
Roland. And do thy worst.
Tranio.   Something I'll do.
Roland.   Do, Tranio. *Exeunt.*

3.2

                    Enter PEDRO *and* JAQUES.

Pedro. A pair of stocks bestride 'em! Are they gone?
Jaques. Yes, they are gone, and all the pans i'th' town
     Beating before 'em. What strange admonitions
     They gave my master, and how fearfully
     They threatened, if he broke 'em!
Pedro.   O' my conscience,   5
     He's found his full match now.
Jaques.   That I believe too.
Pedro. How did she entertain him?
Jaques.   She looked on him –
Pedro. But scurvily?
Jaques.   Faith, with no great affection

---

89. *take . . . way*] (1) be on your way; (2) make the best of it.
walk] go.
90. *fever's off*] mood, humour is passed.
Shalt] Thou shalt.
92. *hurry*] commotion.
93. *works*] deeds, but also alluding to military fortifications.

3.2] Petronius's house.
1. *A . . . 'em*] May they wind up in the stocks (with a vague innuendo on 'bestride').
2–3. *pans . . . Beating*] (The women seem to be beating pans as they march.)
5. *O' my conscience*] (An oath.)
7. *she*] Maria.
8. *scurvily*] in an ugly way.

That I saw, and I heard some say he kissed her,
But 'twas upon a treaty – and some copies   10
Say 'but her cheek'.
Pedro.   Faith, Jaques, what wouldst thou give
For such a wife now?
Jaques.   Full as many prayers
As the most zealous Puritan conceives
(Out of the meditation of fat veal
Or birds of prey, crammed capons) against players,   15
And to as good a tune too, but against her –
That heaven would bless me from her. Mark it, Pedro:
If this house be not turned within this fortnight
With the foundation upward, I'll be carted.
My comfort is yet that those Amorites   20
That came to back her cause, those heathen whores,
Had their hoods hallowed with sack.
Pedro.   How dev'lish drunk they were!
Jaques. And how they tumbled, Pedro! Didst thou mark
The country cavaliero?
Pedro.   Out upon her!
How she turned down the bragget!
Jaques.   Ay, that sunk her.   25
Pedro. That drink was well put to her. What a somersault,
When the chair fell, she fetched, with her heels upward!

---

10. *copies*] reports.

13–15. (Puritans believed that plays and players were sinful. The point is
their hypocrisy in denouncing plays while indulging in gluttony.)

17. *bless . . . her*] i.e., bless me by keeping me from her.

20. *Amorites*] non-monotheistic tribes who inhabited Canaan before the
Israelites.

21. *back*] support.

22. *hoods . . . sack*] (1) hats sprinkled (as with holy water) with wine; (2)
heads blessed with drunkenness (with another ironical suggestion of the
cleric's hood).

24. *cavaliero*] soldier (i.e., the Country Wife).

Out upon her] (An expression of contempt.)

25. *turned . . . bragget*] guzzled the drink made with honey and ale fer-
mented together.

27. *fetched*] made.

Jaques. And what a piece of landscape she discovered!
Pedro. Didst mark her when her hood fell in the posset?
Jaques. Yes, and there rid, like a Dutch hoy. The tumbrel,   30
    When she had got her ballass –
Pedro.   That I saw too.
Jaques. How fain she would have drawn on Sophocles
    To come aboard, and how she simpered it!
Pedro. I warrant her, she has been a worthy striker.
Jaques. I'th' heat of summer, there had been some hope on't,   35
    For then old women are cool cellars.
Pedro.   Hang her!
Jaques. She offered him a Harry-groat, and belched out
    (Her stomach being blown with ale) such courtship,
    Upon my life, has giv'n him twenty stools since.
    Believe my calculation. These old women,   40
    When they are tippled and a little heated,
    Are like new wheels: they'll roar you all the town o'er
    Till they be greased.
Pedro.   The city cinq-a-pas,
    Dame Toast-and-Butter, had her bob too.
Jaques.   Yes,

---

28. *piece*] masterpiece.

landscape] landscape painting, representation of natural scenery. (With ironic reference to her buttocks and/or genitals displayed.)

discovered] uncovered, showed.

29. *posset*] drink of hot milk curdled with ale.

30. *rid*] rode (like a boat in water).

hoy] a small boat. (But also playing on 'whore'.)

tumbrel] flat-bottom barge. (But also playing on 'tumbler' meaning sexual partner.)

31. *ballass*] ballast; balance. (But punning on anatomical *arse*, buttocks.)

33. *come aboard*] i.e., have sex with her.

34. *a worthy striker*] i.e., 'a good lay'.

35. *on't*] of it.

37. *Harry-groat*] a coin stamped with the image of Henry VIII.

38. *blown*] blown up; inflated.

39. *stools*] bowel movements.

41. *tippled*] tipsy.

42. *roar you*] roll rumbling.

43. *cinq-a-pas*] lively five-step dance, here probably a nickname for a 'fast' woman.

44. *bob*] (1) refrain or burden of a song; (2) object with a knob at the end (suggesting the penis); (3) sexual encounter; 'bobbing'.

But she was sullen drunk, and given to filching.   45
I saw her offer at a spoon. – My master!
I do not like his look. I fear he's fasted,
For all this preparation. Let's steal by him.   *Exeunt.*

3.3

Enter PETRUCCIO *and* SOPHOCLES.

Sophocles. Not let you touch her all this night?
Petruccio.   Not touch her.
Sophocles. Where was your courage?
Petruccio.   Where was her obedience?
    Never poor man was shamed so; never rascal
    That keeps a stud of whores was used so basely.
Sophocles. Pray, tell me one thing truly: do you love her?   5
Petruccio. I would I did not, upon that condition
    I passed thee half my land.
Sophocles.   It may be then
    Her modesty required a little violence.
    Some women love to struggle.
Petruccio.   She had it,
    And so much that I sweat for't, so I did;   10
    But to no end. I washed an Ethiop.
    She swore my force might weary her, but win her
    I never could, nor should, till she consented;
    And I might take her body prisoner,

---

45. *filching*] stealing.
46. *offer at*] make an attempt at.
47. *fasted*] i.e., gone without sex.
48. *For*] despite.

3.3] Petruccio and Maria's house.
2. *courage*] (1) strength of will; (2) sexual prowess.
4. *stud*] stable of horses kept for breeding purposes.
used] treated.
6–7. *I . . . land*] I'd give you half my land if I could stop loving her.
6. *would*] wish.
9. *it*] violence.
11. *I washed an Ethiop*] (Eurocentric proverb for an impossible task; an Ethiopian's dark complexion will not be altered by washing.)

But for her mind or appetite –
Sophocles.   'Tis strange.   15
    This woman is the first I ever read of
    Refused a warranted occasion,
    And standing on so fair terms.
Petruccio.   I shall quite her.
Sophocles. Used you no more art?
Petruccio.   Yes, I swore unto her,
    And by no little ones, if presently,   20
    Without more disputation of the matter,
    She grew not nearer to me and dispatched me
    Out of the pain I was (for I was nettled),
    And willingly and eagerly and sweetly,
    I would to her chambermaid and, in her hearing,   25
    Begin her such a hunt's-up.
Sophocles.   Then she startled?
Petruccio. No more than I do now. 'Marry,' she answered,
    If I 'were so disposed,' she 'could not help it;
    But there was one called Jaques, a poor butler,
    One that might well content a single woman'.   30
Sophocles. And he should tilt her?
Petruccio.   To that sense. And last,
    She bade me yet these six months look for nothing,
    Nor strive to purchase it, but fair 'good night'
    And so 'good morrow', and a kiss or two

---

15. *for*] as for.
17. *Refused . . . occasion*] who missed a legitimate sexual opportunity.
18. *standing*] (Allusion to Petruccio's erection.)
quite] requite.
19. *art*] craft; guile.
20. *ones*] oaths. (A line, containing something blasphemous, has probably been lost.)
23. *pain*] emotional distress (but probably also alluding to the discomfort of his erection).
25. *would to*] would go to.
26. *Begin . . . hunt's-up*] i.e., rouse her, get her going. ('The Hunt Is Up' was a song sung to wake the hunters on the morning of the hunt.)
29. *butler*] servant in charge of the wine cellar.
31. *tilt*] (1) joust with; charge or thrust at, as in jousting; (2) have sex with.
To that sense] What she said was to that effect.
32. *look for*] expect.
33. *purchase*] acquire.

To close my stomach – for her vow had sealed it,   35
And she would keep it constant.
Sophocles.   Stay ye, stay.
Was she so when you wooed her?
Petruccio.   Nothing, Sophocles,
More kindly eager. I was oft afraid
She had been light and easy, she would shower
Her kisses so upon me.
Sophocles.   Then I fear   40
Another spoke's i'th' wheel.
Petruccio.   Now thou hast found me.
There gnaws my devil, Sophocles. O Patience,
Preserve me, that I make her not example
By some unworthy way, as flaying her,
Boiling, or making verjuice, drying her –   45
Sophocles. I hear her.
Petruccio.   Mark her then, and see the heir
Of spite and prodigality. She has studied
A way to beggar's both, and, by this hand,
She shall be, if I live, a doxy.

          [*Enter*] MARIA *at the door, and* Servants.

Sophocles.   Fie, sir.
Maria. [*To servants*] I do not like that dressing; 'tis too poor.   50
Let me have six gold laces, broad and massy,
And betwixt ev'ry lace a rich embroidery.
Line the gown through with plush perfumed, and purfle

---

35. *close my stomach*] i.e. stave off my appetite.
sealed it] confirmed the matter.
36. *Stay ye*] Wait a minute.
38. *kindly*] (1) generously; (2) naturally.
39. *light and easy*] loose; lascivious.
41. *Another . . . wheel*] i.e., she is getting sex elsewhere.
thou . . . me] you've figured it out, hit the nail on the head.
42. *There . . . devil*] i.e., That's what is bothering me.
45. *verjuice*] the acid juice of crab-apples, unripe grapes, or other sour fruit, concentrated and used for medicinal purposes.
48. *beggar's*] beggar or impoverish us.
49. *a doxy*] a low-class prostitute.
50. *dressing*] outfit.
51. *massy*] massive.
53. *purfle*] adorn the borders.

All the sleeves down with pearls.
Petruccio.   What think you, Sophocles?
    In what point stands my state now?
Maria. [*To servants*]   For these hangings,   55
    Let 'em be carried where I gave appointment
    (They are too base for my use), and bespeak
    New pieces, of the civil wars of France.
    Let 'em be large and lively, and all silk-work,
    The borders gold.
Sophocles. [*To Petruccio*] Ay, marry, sir, this cuts it.   60
Maria. [*To her servants*] That fourteen yards of satin, give
        my woman.
    I do not like the colour; 'tis too civil.
    There's too much silk i'th' lace too. Tell the Dutchman
    That brought the mares, he must with all speed send me
    Another suit of horses and, by all means,   65
    Ten cast of hawks for th' river. I much care not
    What price they bear, so they be sound and flying,
    For the next winter I am for the country
    And mean to take my pleasure. Where's the horseman?
Petruccio. [*To Sophocles*] She means to ride a great-horse.
Sophocles.   With a side saddle?   70
Petruccio. Yes, and she'll run a-tilt within this twelvemonth.
Maria. [*To horseman*] Tomorrow I'll begin to learn. But
        pray, sir,

---

55. *In . . . state*] In what a situation are my affairs.
For] As for.
56. *where . . . appointment*] where I specified.
57. *bespeak*] order.
58. *pieces*] tapestries.
60. *this cuts it*] (An expression of incredulity; 'this goes too far'.)
61. *woman*] maidservant.
62. *civil*] sombre.
63. *too much silk*] i.e., not enough gold thread, an even *more* precious material.
65. *suit*] set.
66. *cast*] pairs (the number of hawks to be cast or loosed at a time).
67. *so . . . sound*] as long as they are healthy.
68. *for*] going to.
70. *great-horse*] war-horse, charger, considered unsuitable for ladies.
71. *run a-tilt*] (1) joust; (2) act the male role in sex. (Tilt = thrust.)

Have a great care he be an easy doer;
    'Twill spoil a scholar else.
Sophocles. [*To Petruccio*]   An easy doer?
    Did you hear that?
Petruccio.   Yes, I shall meet her morals   75
    Ere it be long, I fear not.   *Exeunt* Servants.
Maria. [*Coming forward to Sophocles*] Oh, good morrow.
Sophocles. Good morrow, lady. How is't now?
Maria.   Faith, sickly.
    This house stands in an ill air –
Petruccio.   Yet more charges!
Maria. Subject to rots and rheums. Out on't! 'Tis nothing
    But a tiled fog.
Petruccio.   What think you of the lodge then?   80
Maria. I like the seat, but 'tis too little. – Sophocles,
    Let me have thy opinion; thou hast judgement.
Petruccio. 'Tis very well.
Maria. [*To Sophocles*]   What if I pluck it down
    And build a square upon it, with two courts
    Still rising from the entrance?
Petruccio.   And i'th' midst   85
    A college for young scolds?
Maria. [*To Sophocles*]   And to the southward
    Take in a garden of some twenty acres
    And cast it of the Italian fashion, hanging?
Petruccio. And you could cast yourself so too! – Pray, lady,
    Will not this cost much money?
Maria.   Some five thousand;   90

---

73. *easy doer*] (1) gentle; easy to ride; (2) 'easy lay'.

74. *scholar*] beginner.

75. *meet her morals*] i.e., sink to her unethical behaviour.

79. *rheums*] aches and pains induced by cold, damp weather.

Out on't] Away with it.

80. *tiled fog*] i.e., not a house, but fog with tiles around it.

lodge] small building at entrance of an estate; gatehouse.

81. *seat*] location.

84. *courts*] courtyards.

85. *Still rising from*] connected to.

87. *Take in*] include.

87–8. *a garden . . . hanging*] (A hanging garden was a garden built above a steep slope or wall, with the growth hanging over the incline.)

89. *cast yourself so*] i.e., commission a bronze of yourself, hanging.

Say six. I'll have it battled too.
Petruccio.   And gilt? Maria,
This is a fearful course you take. Pray, think on't.
You are a woman now, a wife, and his
That must in honesty and justice look for
Some due obedience from you.
Maria.   That bare word   95
Shall cost you many a pound more, build upon't.
Tell me of due obedience! What's a husband?
What are we married for? To carry sumpters?
Are we not one piece with you, and as worthy
Our own intentions as you yours?
Petruccio.   Pray, hear me.   100
Maria. Take two small drops of water, equal weighed:
Tell me which is the heaviest, and which ought
First to descend in duty.
Petruccio.   You mistake me.
I urge not service from you, nor obedience
In way of duty, but of love and credit.   105
All I expect is but a noble care
Of what I have brought you and of what I am
And what our name may be.
Maria.   That's in my making.
Petruccio. 'Tis true, it is so.
Maria.   Yes, it is, Petruccio,
For there was never man – without our moulding,   110
Without our stamp upon him, and our justice –
Left anything three ages after him

---

91. *battled*] embellished with battlements, like a miniature castle. (Maria
describes the country 'great house' increasingly in fashion among the
aristocracy.)

96. *build upon't*] count on it. (But punning on the building she has in
mind.)

97. *Tell me*] Dare you tell me.

98. *sumpters*] saddle-packs.

99. *one piece*] equal. (Also alluding to biblical account of Eve's creation
from Adam's rib.)

105. *credit*] trust.

108. *name*] reputation; family name.

making] (1) nature; (2) control.

110. *our*] women's.

Good and his own.
Sophocles.　　　　　　　Good lady, understand him.
Maria. I do too much, sweet Sophocles. He's one
　　Of a most spiteful self-condition,　　　　　　　　115
　　Never at peace with anything but age,
　　That has no teeth left to return his anger.
　　A bravery dwells in his blood yet of abusing
　　His first good wife; he's sooner fire than powder,
　　And sooner mischief.
Petruccio.　　　　　If I be so sudden,　　　　　　120
　　Do not you fear me?
Maria.　　　　　　No, nor yet care for you –
　　And, if it may be lawful, I defy you.
Petruccio. Does this become you now?
Maria.　　　　　　　　　It shall become me.
Petruccio. Thou disobedient, weak, vainglorious woman,
　　Were I but half so wilful as thou spiteful,　　　　125
　　I should now drag thee to thy duty.
Maria.　　　　　　　　　Drag me!
Petruccio. But I am friends again. Take all your pleasure.
Maria. Now you perceive him, Sophocles.
Petruccio.　　　　　　　　　I love thee
　　Above thy vanity, thou faithless creature.
Maria. [*To Sophocles*] Would I had been so happy, when I
　　　married,　　　　　　　　　　　　　130
　　But to have met an honest man like thee
　　(For I am sure thou art good, I know thou art honest),
　　A handsome hurtless man, a loving man,
　　Though never a penny with him, and these eyes,

---

115. *self-condition*] disposition.
118. *bravery*] pride.
119–20. *sooner . . . mischief*] quicker to explode than gunpowder, and quicker to mischief.
120. *sudden*] impetuous; rash.
127. *Take . . . pleasure*] Have it your way.
128. *perceive him*] see the way he behaves.
129. *Above*] Despite.
130. *happy*] lucky.
133. *hurtless*] harmless.
134. *never . . . him*] without a penny as far as he's concerned.

That face, and that true heart. Wear this for my sake.   135
                              [*She gives him a ring.*]
And, when thou think'st upon me, pity me.
I am cast away.   *Exit.*
Sophocles.   Why, how now, man?
Petruccio.   Pray, leave me,
And follow your advices.
Sophocles. [*Aside*]   The man's jealous.
Petruccio. I shall find a time, ere it be long, to ask you
One or two foolish questions.
Sophocles.   I shall answer   140
As well as I am able, when you call me.
[*Aside*] If she mean true, 'tis but a little killing;
And if I do not venture it, rots take me! –
Farewell, sir.
Petruccio.   Pray, farewell.   *Exit* SOPHOCLES.
                        Is there no keeping
A wife to one man's use? no wintering   145
These cattle without straying? 'Tis hard dealing,
Very hard dealing, gentlemen, strange dealing.
Now, in the name of madness, what star reigned,
What dog-star, bull or bear-star, when I married
This second wife, this whirlwind, that takes all   150
Within her compass? Was I not well warned
(I thought I had, and I believe I know it)
And beaten to repentance in the days
Of my first doting? Had I not wife enough

---

138. *advices*] designs.

141. *call me*] call me out to duel.

142. *but a little*] only a little. (Ironic understatement.)

143. *rots take me*] may I be afflicted with a disease that makes my flesh rot.

146. *straying*] their straying.

147. *gentlemen*] (the men in the audience, or specifically the men seated in the expensive seats on stage).

149. *dog-star . . . bear-star*] Sirius, the dog-star, is the brightest fixed star; it was believed to produce the suffocating 'dog-days' of August. (Petruccio also alludes to the constellations of Taurus, the bull, and Ursa Major, the bear.)

151. *compass*] control, vicinity.

152. *had*] had been.

154. *doting*] excessive love for a woman.

To turn my tools to? Did I want vexation   155
Or any special care to kill my heart?
Had I not ev'ry morning a rare breakfast
Mixed with a learnèd lecture of ill language
Louder than Tom o' Lincoln, and at dinner
A diet of the same dish? Was there evening   160
That e'er passed over us without 'thou knave'
Or 'thou whore' for digestion? Had I ever
A pull at this same poor sport men run mad for
But like a cur I was fain to show my teeth first
And almost worry her? And did heaven forgive me   165
And take this serpent from me, and am I
Keeping tame devils now again? My heart aches.
Something I must do speedily. I'll die,
If I can handsomely, for that's the way
To make a rascal of her. I am sick,   170
And I'll go very near it, but I'll perish.   *Exit.*

3.4

Enter LIVIA, BIANCA, ROLAND, *and* TRANIO.

Livia. Then I must be content, sir, with my fortune.
Roland. And I with mine.
Livia.   I did not think a look
   Or a poor word or two could have displanted
   Such a fixed constancy, and for your end too.

---

155. *turn . . . to*] work on. (With sexual innuendo: *tools* = 'genitals'.)
   want] lack.
   157. *rare*] special. (Sarcastic.)
   159. *Tom o' Lincoln*] the great bell in Lincoln Cathedral; also the subject of a popular romance and a play.
   163. *pull*] go.
   sport] sex.
   164. *cur*] ill-tempered dog.
   165. *worry*] seize by the throat with the teeth, as hounds do their quarry.
   169. *can*] can do so.
   171.] I'll come as close as I can to winning, or die in the attempt.

   3.4] Petronius's house.
   4. *for your end*] i.e., on your behalf, or, for your own part.

Roland. Come, come, I know your courses. There's your
    gewgaws,   5
  Your rings and bracelets and the purse you gave me;
  The money's spent in entertaining you
  At plays and cherry gardens.
               [They exchange former love-tokens.]
Livia.   There's your chain too.
  But, if you'll give me leave, I'll wear the hair still;
  I would yet remember you.
Bianca.   Give him his lock, wench.   10
  The young man has employment for't.
            [Roland takes the lock of hair from Livia.]
Tranio.   Fie, Roland!
Roland. You cannot fie me out a hundred pound
  With this poor plot. *[Aside]* Yet let me ne'er see day more
  If something do not struggle strangely in me.
Bianca. Young man, let me talk with you.
Roland.   Well, young woman?   15
Bianca. This was your mistress once.
Roland.   Yes.
Bianca.   Are ye honest?
  I see you are young and handsome.
Roland.   I am honest.
Bianca. Why, that's well said. And there's no doubt your
    judgement
  Is good enough and strong enough to tell you
  Who are your foes and friends. Why did you leave her?   20
Roland. She made a puppy of me.
Bianca.   Be that granted.
  She must do so sometimes, and oftentimes;
  Love were too serious else.
Roland.   A witty woman!

---

5. *gewgaws*] trinkets.
7. *money's spent*] (She gave him a full purse; he returns it empty.)
9. *hair*] hair in the locket.
10–11. *Give . . . for't*] i.e., Let him go; he'll find someone else to love.
13. *ne'er . . . more*] i.e., live.
23. *else*] otherwise.

Bianca. Had ye loved *me* –
Roland.   I would I had.
Bianca.   – and dearly,
 And I had loved you so – you may love worse, sir.   25
 But that is not material.
Roland. [*Aside*]   I shall lose.
Bianca. Some time or other, for variety,
 I should have called ye fool or boy, or bid ye
 Play with the pages, but have loved you still,
 Out of all question, and extremely too.   30
 You are a man made to be loved.
Roland. [*Aside*]   This woman
 Either abuses me or loves me dearly.
Bianca. I'll tell you one thing: if I were to choose
 A husband to my own mind, I should think
 One of your mother's making would content me,   35
 For, o' my conscience, she gets good ones.
Roland.   Lady,
 I'll leave you to your commendations.
 [*Aside*] I am in again. The devil take their tongues!
Bianca. You shall not go.
Roland.   I will. – Yet thus far, Livia:
 Your sorrow may induce me to forgive ye,   40
 But never love again. [*Aside*] If I stay longer,
 I have lost two hundred pound.
Livia.   Good sir, but thus much.
Tranio. [*To Roland*] Turn, if thou be'st a man.
Livia. [*To Roland*]   But one kiss of ye,
 One parting kiss, and I am gone too.
Roland.   Come.
 [*Aside*] I shall kiss fifty pound away at this clap. –   45
 We'll have one more, and then farewell. *He kisses Livia.*
Livia.   Farewell, sir.
Bianca. [*To Roland*] Well, go thy ways. Thou bear'st a kind
 heart with thee.

---

 26. *lose*] i.e., lose the bet not to fall in love a second time.
 32. *abuses*] deceives.
 34. *my own mind*] my tastes.
 36. *gets*] begets, gives birth to.
 38. *in*] i.e., 'in deep'; falling for it.

Tranio. He's made a stand.

Bianca.   A noble brave young fellow,
    Worthy a wench indeed.

Roland.   I will – I will not.   *Exit.*

Tranio. [*To Livia*] Is gone, but shot again. Play you but your
        part   50
    And I will keep my promise. Forty angels
    In fair gold, lady – wipe your eyes – he's yours,
    If I have any wit.

Livia.   I'll pay the forfeit.

Bianca. Come then, let's see your sister, how she fares now
    After her skirmish, and be sure Moroso   55
    Be kept in good hand; then all's perfect, Livia.   *Exeunt.*

3.5

            Enter JAQUES *and* PEDRO.

Pedro. O Jaques, Jaques, what becomes of us?
    O my sweet master!

Jaques.   Run for a physician
    And a whole peck of 'pothecaries, Pedro.
    'He will die, diddle, diddle, die' if they come not quickly.
    And bring all empirics straight, and mountebanks,   5
    Skilful in lungs and livers. Raise the neighbours
    And all the aquavitae bottles extant
    And oh, the parson, Pedro, oh, the parson,

---

50. *shot again*] (with Cupid's arrow).

51. *angels*] gold coins.

53. *I'll . . . forfeit*] (If Tranio succeeds, she will pay him the forty angels.)

56. *in good hand*] in control.

3.5] In front of Petruccio and Maria's house.

1. *becomes*] will become.

3. *'pothecaries*] apothecaries; druggists.

4. *'diddle, diddle die'*] ('Diddle, diddle' was a musical jingle; Jaques either quotes an old ballad or improvises one of his own.)

5. *empirics*] ancient physicians who based their methods on direct observation, rather than on doctrine; the term was also used for quacks.

mountebanks] quack doctors who peddled their wares on street-corners, using juggling and clowning to draw a crowd.

7. *aquavitae*] alcoholic restorative.

A little of his comfort, never so little.
Twenty to one you find him at the Bush;   10
There's the best ale.
Pedro.   I fly!   *Exit.*

Enter MARIA, *and* Servants *carrying out household stuff*
and trunks.

Maria.   Out with the trunks, ho!
Why are you idle? Sirrah, up to th' chamber
And take the hangings down, and see the linen
Packed up and sent away within this half hour.
What, are the carts come yet? Some honest body   15
Help down the chests of plate, and some the wardrobe.
Alas, we are undone else!
Jaques.   Pray, forsooth,
And I beseech ye, tell me, is 'a dead yet?
Maria. No, but is drawing on. – Out with the armour!
Jaques. Then I'll go see him.
Maria.   Thou art undone then, fellow.   20
No man that has been near him come near me.

Enter SOPHOCLES *and* PETRONIUS.

Sophocles. Why, how now, lady? What means this?
Petronius.   Now, daughter!
How does my son?
Maria.   Save all ye can, for [God's] sake!

Enter LIVIA, BIANCA, *and* TRANIO.

Livia. Be of good comfort, sister.
Maria.   Oh, my casket!
Petronius. How does thy husband, woman?
Maria.   Get ye gone,   25

---

9. *never so little*] as much as can be.
10. *the Bush*] a tavern.
12. *Sirrah*] (A term of address for a social subordinate.)
15. *honest body*] good person.
16. *down*] carry down.
18. *'a*] he.
19. *drawing on*] i.e., approaching death.
armour] suit of armour (family heirloom proving distinguished ancestry).
23. *son*] son-in-law.

If you mean to save your lives. The sickness –
Petronius. Stand further off, I prithee.
Maria.　　　　　　　　　　Is i'th' house, sir.
My husband has it now, and raves extremely!
Give me some counsel, friends.
Bianca.　　　　　　　　Why, lock the doors up
And send him in a woman to attend him.　　　　　30
Maria. I have bespoke two women, and the city
Has sent a watch, I thank 'em. Meat nor money
He shall not want, nor prayers.
Petronius.　　　　　　　How long is't
Since it first took him?
Maria.　　　　　　　But within this three hours.

Enter the Watchmen.

I am frighted from my wits, my friends. – The watch!　　35
Pray, do your office. Lock the doors up fast.
And patience be his angel!　　　*They lock the door.*
Tranio.　　　　　　This comes unlooked for.
Maria. I'll to the lodge. Some, that are kind and love me,
I know will visit me.
Petruccio. (*Within*)　　Do you hear, my masters?
Ho, you that lock the doors up!
Petronius.　　　　　　'Tis his voice.　　　　40
Tranio. Hold, and let's hear him.
Petruccio. [*Within*]　　　Will ye starve me here?
Am I a traitor or an heretic?
Or am I grown infectious?
Petronius.　　　　　Pray, sir, pray!
Petruccio. [*Within*] I am as well as you are, goodman puppy.

---

26. *sickness*] plague (endemic in London, 1603–10).
31. *bespoke*] summoned, engaged.
32. *watch*] watchmen.
32–3. *Meat . . . prayers*] i.e., He shall not lack food, money, or prayers.
33. *is't*] has it been.
35. *from*] out of.
36. *fast*] tight.
41. *Hold*] Hold off.
44. *goodman*] A title for a non-gentleman (thus, deliberately patronizing here).

Maria. Pray, have patience.   45
    You shall want nothing, sir.
Petruccio. [*Within*]   I want a cudgel
    And thee, thou wickedness!
Petronius. [*To Maria*]   He speaks well enough.
Maria. Had ever a strong heart, sir.
Petruccio. [*Within*]   Will ye hear me? First, be pleased
    To think I know ye all, and can distinguish
    Ev'ry man's several voice. You that spoke first   50
    I know my father-in-law; the other, Tranio;
    And I heard Sophocles; the last – pray, mark me –
    Is my damned wife Maria. Gentlemen!
    'Death, gentlemen, do ye make a May-game on me?
    I tell ye once again, I am as sound,   55
    As well, as wholesome, and as sensible
    As any of ye all. Let me out quickly
    Or, as I am a man, I'll beat the walls down,
    And the first thing I light upon shall pay for't.
Petronius. Fetch a doctor presently, and if   60
    He can do no good on him, he must to Bedlam.
Petruccio. [*Within*] Will it please ye open?
Tranio. His fit grows stronger still.
Maria. Let's save ourselves, sir.
    He's past all worldly cure.
Petronius. [*To the Watch*]   Friends, do your office.   65
    And what he wants – if money, love, or labour,

---

   46. *want*] (This line quibbles on the sense of 'want' as to need and to
desire.)
   48. *Had*] He had.
   50. *several*] distinct.
   51. *know*] know as.
   54. *'Death*] God's death. (A strong oath.)
   May-game] (May-day festivities involved various tricks and games.)
   56. *wholesome*] free of plague.
   sensible] sane.
   59. *light*] come.
   61. *on*] for.
   he . . . Bedlam] he must be sent to the hospital of St Mary of
Bethlehem, a lunatic asylum.
   on] for.
   65. *office*] duty.
   66. *what*] whatever.

Or any way, may win it – let him have it.
Farewell, and pray, my honest friends.

Exeunt. Manent Watchmen.

Petruccio. [*Within*]　　　　　　　　Why, rascals!
　　Friends! Gentlemen! Thou beastly wife! Jaques!
　　None hear me? Who's at the door there?
First Watchman.　　　　　　　　Think, I pray, sir,　　70
　　Whither ye are going, and prepare yourself.
Second Watchman. [*To Petruccio*] These idle thoughts disturb
　　　　ye. The good gentlewoman,
　　Your wife, has taken care ye shall want nothing.
Petruccio. [*Within*] The blessing of her grandam Eve light on
　　　　her!
　　Nothing but thin fig leaves, to hide her knavery!　　75
　　Shall I come out in quiet? – answer me –
　　Or shall I charge a fowling-piece, and make
　　Mine own way? Two of ye I cannot miss,
　　If I miss three. Ye come here to assault me!
First Watchman. There's onions roasting for your sore, sir.
Petruccio. [*Within*]　　　　　　　　People,　　80
　　I am as excellent well, I thank [God] for't,
　　And have as good a stomach at this instant –
Second Watchman. That's an ill sign.
First Watchman.　　　　　　He draws on; he's a dead man.
Petruccio. [*Within*] And sleep as soundly – will ye look upon
　　　　me?
First Watchman. Do ye want pen and ink? While ye have
　　sense, sir,　　85

---

68. SD Manent] (Latin) They remain.

71. *Whither . . . going*] i.e., to heaven or hell.

74. *blessing . . . Eve*] Eve's curse was subordination to her husband and pain in childbirth; both Adam and Eve first suffered shame of their nakedness as a result of the fall.

76. *in quiet*] i.e., in peace.

77. *fowling-piece*] shotgun.

79. *If . . . three*] even if I miss three others.

80. *onions*] (to make a poultice).

82. *stomach*] appetite.

83. *draws on*] nears death.

85. *have sense*] are conscious.

Settle your state.

Petruccio. [*Within*]   Sirs, I am as well as you are,
Or any rascal living.

First Watchman.   Would ye were, sir!

Petruccio. [*Within*] Look to yourselves, and – if ye love your
     lives –
Open the door and fly me, for I shoot else.
[God's light,] I'll shoot, and presently, chain-bullets,   90
And under four I will not kill.

Second Watchman. [*To others*]   Let's quit him.
It may be it is a trick; he's dangerous.

First Watchman. The devil take the hindmost, I cry!

                              Exeunt [Watchmen], *running.*

Petruccio. [*Within*]   Have among ye!
The door shall open too. I'll have a fair shot.

     Enter PETRUCCIO *with a piece, and forces the door open.*

Are ye all gone? Tricks in my old days, crackers   95
Put now upon me? And by Lady Greensleeves?
Am I grown so tame after all my triumphs?
But that I should be thought mad, if I railed
As much as they deserve against these women,
I would now rip up, from the primitive cuckold,   100
All their arch villainies and all their doubles,
Which are more than a hunted hare e'er thought on.
When a man has the fairest and the sweetest
Of all their sex and, as he thinks, the noblest,

---

86. *state*] estate.

90. *God's light*] (A strong oath; alluding to God's 'Let there be light' in
Genesis.)

chain-bullets] chain-shots; bullets joined by chains.

91. *under . . . kill*] I'll kill at least four.

quit] leave.

93. *Have among ye!*] Here I come! Watch out!

95. *crackers*] lies.

96. *Lady Greensleeves*] inconstant lady, subject of a popular ballad. (Referring here to Maria.)

98. *But that*] Were it not that.

100. *rip up*] expose and denounce.

primitive] first.

101. *doubles*] evasions, like a hunted animal that doubles back across its
own track, so that pursuing dogs will lose the scent.

What has he then? And I'll speak modestly: 105
He has a quartern-ague, that shall shake
All his estate to nothing, never cured,
Nor never dying; has a ship to venture
His fame and credit in, which – if 'a man not
With more continual labour than a galley,   110
To make her tilth – either she grows a tumbrel,
Not worth the cloth she wears, or springs more leaks
Than all the fame of his posterity
Can ever stop again. Out on 'em, hedgehogs!
He that shall touch 'em has a thousand thorns   115
Runs through his fingers. If I were unmarried,
I would do anything below repentance,
Any base dunghill slavery, be a hangman,
Ere I would be a husband. Oh, the thousand,
Thousand, ten thousand ways they have to kill us!   120
Some fall with too much stringing of the fiddles,
And those are fools; some, that they are not suffered,
And those are maudlin lovers; some, like scorpions,
They poison with their tails, and those are martyrs;
Some die with doing good, those benefactors,   125
And leave 'em land to leap away; some few,
For those are rarest, they are said to kill

---

106. *quartern-ague*] violent fever.

109–10. *'a man . . . labour*] he does not continually sexually satisfy (*'a* =
he; *man* is a verb).

110. *galley*] ship rowed by slaves chained to their benches. (Considered
the worst form of slavery.)

111. *tilth*] yield a crop (i.e., give birth).

tumbrel] (1) flat-bottomed barge; (2) person who is falling-down drunk.

112. *leaks*] (referring to venereal disease).

114–30. *Out . . . upwards*] (Cut in Caroline performances.)

114. *hedgehogs*] i.e., prickly creatures.

117. *below*] short of.

121.] i.e., Some men are outworn by women's voracious sexual appetites.
(The fiddle and bow represent the female and male sex organs, respectively.)

122. *not suffered*] not permitted (to have sex).

123–4. *like scorpions . . . martyrs*] some women (like scorpions) poison
men with their tails (genitals); i.e., they give men venereal disease, and thus
martyr them (torture and/or kill them).

126. *leap away*] squander through dancing and other frivolity (including
sexually mounting men).

With kindness and fair usage; but what they are
My catalogue discovers not, only 'tis thought
They are buried in old walls, with their heels upward.   130
I could rail twenty days together now!
I'll seek 'em out, and – if I have not reason,
And very sensible, why this was done –
I'll go a-birding yet, and some shall smart for't.   *Exit.*

---

130. *buried . . . upward*] i.e., buried outside of consecrated ground, in an
undignified (sexually suggestive) position.

131. *rail*] scold.

134. *a-birding*] bird-hunting, i.e., chasing after chicks.

Act 4

Enter PETRUCCIO, JAQUES, *and* PEDRO.

Jaques. [*To Petruccio*] And, as I told Your Worship, all the
    hangings,
    Brass, pewter, plate, ev'n to the very pisspots.
Pedro. [*To Petruccio*] And that that hung for our defence, the
    armour,
    And the March-beer was going too. – Oh, Jaques,
    What a sad sight was that!
Jaques. [*To Petruccio*]   Even the two rundlets,   5
    The two that was our hope, of muscatel –
    Better, ne'er tongue tripped over – those two cannons
    To batter brawn withal at Christmas, sir,
    Ev'n those two lovely twins, the enemy
    Had almost cut off clean.
Petruccio.   Go trim the house up   10
    And put the things in order as they were.
    I shall find time for all this. *Exeunt* JAQUES *and* PEDRO.
                    Could I find her
    But constant any way, I had done my business.
    Were she a whore directly, or a scold,
    An unthrift, or a woman made to hate me,   15

4.1] In front of Petruccio and Maria's house. For the additional scene
originally found here see Appendix.
  3. *that that hung for*] that which was hung for.
  4. *March-beer*] strong beer brewed in March.
  5. *rundlets*] casks.
  7. *Better . . . over*] No better wine ever made a tongue trip with tipsiness.
  7–8. *cannons . . . Christmas*] (The metaphor compares wine-barrels to
heavy artillery: the enemy is a roast pig ['brawn'] to be figuratively attacked
at Christmas.)
  10. *cut off*] finished off, or cut off of something or someone.
  14. *directly*] overtly.
  15. *unthrift*] spend-thrift; prodigal.

    I had my wish, and knew which way to rein her.
    But while she shows all these, and all their losses,
    A kind of linsey-wolsey mingled mischief
    Not to be guessed at, and whether true or borrowed
    Not certain neither – what a hap had I,   20

Enter MARIA [*apart*].

    And what a tidy fortune, when my fate
    Flung me upon this bear-whelp! Here she comes.
    Now, if she have a colour for this fault –
    A cleanly one, upon my conscience –
    I shall forgive her yet, and find a something   25
    Certain I married for, her wit. I'll mark her.
Maria. Not let his wife come near him in his sickness?
    Not come to comfort him? She that all laws
    Of heaven and nations have ordained his second,
    Is she refused? And two old paradoxes,   30
    Pieces of five-and-fifty, without faith,
    Clapped in upon him? Has a little pet,
    That all young wives must follow necessary,
    Having their maidenheads –
Petruccio. [*Aside*]   This is an axiom
    I never heard before.
Maria.   Or say rebellion,   35

---

17. *shows . . . losses*] demonstrates all these flaws at once, and simultaneously the lack of them (she both is and is not acting shrewish).

18. *linsey-wolsey*] a textile made of mixed wool and flax; hence, a strange combination.

20. *what a hap*] what luck. (Ironic.)

22. *bear-whelp*] bear-cub.

23. *colour*] excuse.

24. *cleanly*] chaste; decent.

29. *his second*] his second self, 'other half'.

30. *old paradoxes*] literally 'traditional self-contradictory statement' ('Zeno's paradox', etc.); the women are living paradoxes, absurdly, fantastically ancient.

31. *Pieces*] women. (Derogatory.)
faith] religion.

32. *Clapped . . . him*] locked in with him.
pet] fit of ill-humour.

33. *necessary*] necessarily; obligatorily.

34. *axiom*] proposition; maxim.

If we durst be so foul – which two fair words,
Alas, win us from in an hour, an instant,
We are so easy – made him so forgetful
Both of his reason, honesty, and credit,
As to deny his wife a visitation?   40
His wife that, though she was a little foolish,
Loved him – O heaven, forgive her for't! – nay, doted,
Nay, had run mad, had she not married him.

Petruccio. [*Aside*] Though I do know this falser than the devil,
I cannot choose but love it.

Maria.   What do I know   45
But those that came to keep him might have killed him?
In what a case had I been then? I dare not
Believe him such a base debauched companion
That one refusal of a tender maid
Would make him feign this sickness out of need,   50
And take a keeper to him of fourscore
To play at billiards, one that mewed content
And all her teeth together. Not come near him?

Petruccio. [*Aside*] This woman would have made a most rare
    Jesuit.
She can prevaricate on anything.   55
There was not to be thought a way to save her,
In all imagination, beside this.

Maria. His unkind meaning, which was worst of all,
In sending, [God] knows whither, all the plate
And all the household stuff, had I not crossed it,   60
By a great providence and my friends' assistance,
Which he will thank me one day for. Alas,

---

36. *durst . . . foul*] dare be so insolent.
36–8. *fair . . . easy*] kind words would quell, as we are so docile.
37. *win vs from*] persuade us to abandon.
46. *But*] But that.
47. *case*] situation.
52–3. *mewed . . . together*] lost her teeth and her pleasure at once.
53. *Not come*] Am I not allowed to come.
54. *rare Jesuit*] excellent Jesuit. (Jesuits were stereotypically smooth talkers and subversives.)
55. *prevaricate*] equivocate; talk evasively.
56–7.] One couldn't possibly imagine a better excuse than this.
60. *crossed*] thwarted.

I could have watched as well as they, have served him
In any use better and willinger.
The law commands me do it, love commands me,   65
And my own duty charges me.
Petruccio. [*Aside*]   [God] bless me!
And, now I have said my prayers, I'll go to her. –
Are you a wife for any man?
Maria.   For you, sir,
If I were worse, I were better. That ye are well,
At least that ye appear so, I thank heaven.   70
Long may it hold! And that you are here, I am glad too.
But that you have abused me wretchedly,
And such a way that shames the name of husband,
Such a malicious mangy way, so mingled –
Never look strangely on me; I dare tell you –   75
With breach of honesty, care, kindness, manners –
Petruccio. Holla! ye kick too fast.
Maria.   Was I a stranger?
Or had I vowed perdition to your person?
Am I not married to you? Tell me that.
Petruccio. I would I could not tell you.
Maria.   Is my presence,   80
The stock I come of, which is worshipful –
If I should say 'right worshipful', I lied not;
My grandsire was a knight –
Petruccio.   O'th' shire?
Maria.   A soldier,
Which none of all thy family e'er heard of,

---

63. *watched . . . they*] watched over him as well as the old women.

69. *If . . . better*] i.e., A 'worse' wife (one even more stern than I am) would be better for you.

71. *hold*] last.

74. *mangy*] shabby (literally, afflicted with the mange, a scabby skin condition).

77. *Holla!*] Whoah!

78. *perdition*] harm.

81. *worshipful*] honourable.

83. *grandsire*] grandfather.

knight O'th' shire] country gentleman representing a shire or county (as opposed to a soldier, knighted for conspicuous valour).

84. *heard of*] could boast of.

But one conductor of thy name, a grazier   85
That ran away wi'th' pay. Or am I grown,
Because I have been a little peevish to you,
Only to try your temper, such a dog-leech
I could not be admitted to your presence?
Petruccio. If I endure this, hang me.
Maria.   And two death's heads,   90
Two Harry-groats that had their faces worn,
Almost their names away too –
Petruccio.   Now hear me,
For I will stay no longer.
Maria.   This you shall:
However you shall think to flatter me
For this offence – which no submission   95
Can ever mediate for; you'll find it so –
Whatever ye shall do by intercession,
What ye can offer, what your land can purchase,
What all your friends or family can win,
Shall be but this, not to forswear your knowledge,   100
But ever to forbear it. Now your will, sir.
Petruccio. Thou art the subtlest woman, I think, living;
I am sure, the lewdest. Now be still, and mark me.
Were I but any way addicted to the devil,
I should now think I had met a playfellow   105

---

85. *conductor*] bearer.

grazier] one who feeds cattle to fatten them for market.

86. *wi'th' pay*] with the payroll.

88. *try*] test.

dog-leech] (1) veterinarian who treats dogs; (2) quack doctor.

91–2. *Harry-groats*] coins minted in the early sixteenth century (figuratively, old women with faces worn past recognition – possibly also punning on 'hairy').

93. *This you shall*] i.e., You shall stay and hear me out.

96. *mediate*] atone.

98. *What*] whatever.

100–1. *not . . . it*] not to falsely deny having wronged me, but to do so no more.

101. *your will*] say what you wish.

102. *subtlest*] most wily; most guileful.

103. *sure . . . lewdest*] certainly you are the most lascivious.

104. *addicted*] devoted.

To profit by, and that way the most learnèd
That ever taught to murmur. Tell me, thou,
Thou most poor, paltry, spiteful whore – do you cry?
I'll make you roar, before I leave.

Maria.   Your pleasure.

Petruccio. Was it not sin enough, thou fruiterer   110
Full of the fall thou eat'st, thou devil's broker,
Thou seminary of all sedition,
Thou sword of vengeance with a thread hung o'er us,
Was it not sin enough and wickedness
In full abundance, was it not vexation   115
At all points, *cap-a-pè* – nay, I shall pinch ye –
Thus like a rotten rascal to abuse
The name of heaven, the tie of marriage,
The honour of thy friends, the expectation
Of all that thought thee virtuous, with rebellion,   120
Childish and base rebellion? But continuing –
After forgiveness too – and worse, your mischief?
And against him, setting the hope of heaven by
And the dear reservation of his honour,
Nothing above ground could have won to hate thee?   125
Well, go thy ways.

Maria. [*Going*]   Yes.

Petruccio.   You shall hear me out first.
What punishment mayst thou deserve, thou thing,
Thou idle thing of nothing, thou pulled primrose
That two hours after art a weed and withered,

106–7. *that . . . murmur*] i.e., the most cunning and eloquent instructor of
evil who ever spoke.

109. *Your pleasure*] As you wish.

110. *fruiterer*] fruit-seller. (Alluding to Eve.)

111. *fall*] sin.

113. *sword . . . us*] (Alluding to the sword of Damocles.)

116. *At all points*] in every way.

cap-a-pè] head to foot.

124. *reservation*] preservation.

125. *above ground*] on earth.

126. *go thy ways*] go head, persevere in your ways. (But Maria wilfully
interprets this as an invitation for her to leave.)

128. *pulled*] picked.

For this last flourish on me? Am I one,   130
Selected out of all the husbands living,
To be so ridden by a tit of tenpence?
Am I so blind and bed-rid? I was mad
And had the plague and no man must come near me!
I must be shut up, and my substance 'bezzled,   135
And an old woman watch me!
Maria.   Well, sir, well,
You may well glory in't.
Petruccio. And when it comes to opening, 'tis my plot!
I must undo myself, forsooth! Dost hear me?
If I should beat thee now as much as may be,   140
Dost thou not well deserve it, o' thy conscience,
Dost thou not cry 'Come beat me'?
Maria.   I defy you.
And, my last loving tears, farewell. The first stroke,
The very first you give me, if you dare strike –
Try me, and you shall find it so – for ever,   145
Never to be recalled – I know you love me,
Mad till you have enjoyed me – do I turn
Utterly from you. And what man I meet first,
That has but spirit to deserve a favour,
Let him bear any shape, the worse the better,   150
Shall kill you and enjoy me. What I have said
About your foolish sickness, ere you have me
As you would have me, you shall swear is certain,
And challenge any man that dares deny it,
And in all companies approve my actions.   155
And so farewell for this time.   *Exit.*
Petruccio.   Grief go with thee! –
If there be any witchcrafts, herbs, or potions,

---

130. *flourish on*] defiance of. (A flourish can be a brandishing of the sword or a boast.)
132. *tit of tenpence*] two-bit hussy.
135. *substance 'bezzled*] possessions embezzled or carried away.
137. *glory*] gloat; triumph.
138. *opening*] revealing all.
140. *may be*] possible.
141. *o'*] in, if you examine.

Saying my prayers backward, fiends or fairies,
That can again unlove me, I am made.   *Exit.*

4.2

Enter BIANCA *and* TRANIO.

Tranio. Faith, mistress, you must do it.
Bianca.   Are the writings
    Ready I told ye of?
Tranio.   Yes, they are ready,
    But to what use I know not.
Bianca.   You're an ass.
    You must have all things construed.
Tranio.   Yes, and pierced too,
    Or I find little pleasure.
Bianca.   Now you are knavish.   5
    Go to. Fetch Roland hither presently.
    Your twenty pound lies bleeding else. She is married
    Within these twelve hours, if we cross it not. –
    And see the papers of one size.
Tranio.   I have ye.
Bianca. And for disposing of 'em –
Tranio.   If I fail ye,   10
    Now I have found the way, use martial law
    And cut my head off with a hand-saw.
Bianca.   Well, sir,
    Petronius and Moroso I'll see sent for.

---

159. *unlove me*] i.e., cure me of love.
made] a success.

4.2] Petronius's house.
4 *construed*] explained. (Accented on first syllable; Tranio seizes on the
pun *con* = 'cunt'.)
pierced] (1) penetrated intellectually; (2) penetrated sexually.
5. *knavish*] naughty.
6. *Go to*] (An expression of impatience.)
9. *see . . . size*] see to it that the papers are the same size (and hence can
be switched).
have] understand.
11. *found the way*] grasped the plot.

About your business, go.

Tranio.   I am gone.   *Exit.*

Bianca.   Ho, Livia!

Enter LIVIA.

Livia. Who's that?

Bianca.   A friend of yours. Lord, how you look now,   15
   As if you had lost a carrack.

Livia.   Oh, Bianca,
   I am the most undone, unhappy woman!

Bianca. Be quiet, wench. Thou shalt be done and done
   And done and double done, or all shall split for't.
   No more of these minced passions; they are mangy   20
   And ease thee of nothing but a little wind;
   An apple will do more. Thou fear'st Moroso?

Livia. E'en as I fear the gallows.

Bianca.   Keep thee there still.
   And you love Roland? Say.

Livia.   If I say not,
   I am sure I lie.

Bianca.   What wouldst thou give that woman,   25
   In spite of all his anger and thy fear
   And all thy father's policy, that could
   Clap ye within these two nights quietly
   Into a bed together?

Livia.   How?

Bianca.   Why, fairly,
   At half-sword, man and wife. Now the red blood comes: 30

---

16. *carrack*] large ship used in trading; a galleon.

19. *split*] suffer; with a sexual innuendo. (The split hull of a shipwreck was a metaphor for the sexual broaching of the female 'vessel'.)

20. *minced*] affected.

22. *apple*] (acting as a laxative).

23. *Keep . . . still*] Hold to that.

26. *his*] Moroso's.

27. *policy*] plotting.

28. *Clap*] put.

30. *At half-sword*] at close-quarters, like opponents one half a sword's length apart.

   red blood comes] (Livia is blushing).

Ay, marry, now the matter's changed.

Livia.   Bianca,
    Methinks you should not mock me.

Bianca.   Mock a pudding!
    I speak good honest English, and good meaning.

Livia. I should not be ungrateful to that woman.

Bianca. I know thou wouldst not. Follow but my counsel   35
    And, if thou hast him not, despite of fortune,
    Let me never know a good night more. You must
    Be very sick o'th' instant.

Livia.   Well, what follows?

Bianca. And in that sickness send for all your friends,
    Your father, and your fever, old Moroso;   40
    And Roland shall be there too.

Livia.   What of this?

Bianca. Do ye not twitter yet? Of this shall follow
    That that shall make thy heart leap and thy lips
    Venture as many kisses as the merchants
    Do dollars to the East Indies. You shall know all –   45
    But first walk in and practise. Pray, be sick.

Livia. I do believe ye, and I am sick.

Bianca.   So.
    To bed, then, come. I'll send away your servants,
    Post for your fool and father. And good fortune,
    As we mean honestly, now strike an upshot!   *Exeunt.*   50

---

32. *Mock a pudding!*] Pooh! (Pudding can mean sausage; hence, a phallic pun is possible.)

37. *know . . . night*] i.e., have good sex.

38. *Be*] pretend to be.
o'th' instant] suddenly.

40. *fever*] (1) affliction; (2) Moroso.

41. *What of this?*] i.e., Why all this?

42. *twitter*] tremble with anticipation.

45. *dollars*] English name for the peso, or piece of eight, formerly in use in Spain and the Spanish-American colonies, and hence as an international currency.

46. *practise*] connive; deceive; play a trick.

49. *Post for*] go get.
fool] Moroso.

49–50. *good . . . upshot!*] May fortune strike the final blow for us! (An upshot is the final shot in archery.)

4.3

Enter TRANIO *and* ROLAND.

Tranio. Nay, o' my conscience, I have lost my money.
      But that's all one. I'll never more persuade ye.
      I see you are resolute, and I commend ye.
Roland. But did she send for me?
Tranio.   Ye dare believe me?
Roland. I cannot tell. You have your ways for profit   5
      Allowed ye, Tranio, as well as I
      Have (to avoid 'em) fear.
Tranio.   No, [o' God's name], sir,
      I deal directly with ye.

            Enter Servant [*of Petronius*] *hastily.*

Roland.   How now, fellow?
      Whither post you so fast?
Servant.   Oh, sir, my master,
      Pray, did you see my master?
Roland.   Why your master?   10
Servant. Oh, sir, his jewel –
Roland.   With the gilded button?
Servant. My pretty mistress Livia –
Roland.   What of her?
Servant. Is fallen sick o'th' sudden –
Roland.   How, o'th' sullens?
Servant. O'th' *sudden*, sir, I say, and very sick.
Roland. It seems she hath got the toothache with raw apples.   15
Servant. It seems you have got the headache. Fare ye well, sir.
      You did not see my master?
Roland.   Who told you so?
Tranio. [*To Servant*] No, no, he did not see him.
Roland. [*To Servant*]   Farewell, blue-bottle.
                                              Exit Servant.

4.3] Somewhere in London.
2. *that's all one*] never mind.
9. *post*] rush.
13. *sullens*] melancholy. (Playing on sudden/sullens.)
15. *apples*] (which would dislocate unhealthy teeth).
18. *blue-bottle*] (Referring to the servant's blue uniform.)

What should her sickness be?

Tranio.   For you, it may be.

Roland. Yes, when my brains are out, I may believe it;   20
  Never before, I am sure. Yet I may see her;
  'Twill be a point of honesty.

Tranio.   It will so.

Roland. It may be not, too. You would fain be fing'ring
  This old sin-off'ring of two hundred, Tranio.
  How daintily and cunningly you drive me   25
  Up like a deer to th' toil! Yet I may leap it –
  And what's the woodman then?

Tranio.   A loser, by ye.
  Speak, will you go or not? To me 'tis equal.

Roland. Come, what goes less?

Tranio.   Nay, not a penny, Roland.

Roland. Shall I have liberty of conscience   30
  Which, by interpretation, is ten kisses?
  Hang me if I affect her. Yet it may be
  This whoreson manners will require a struggling
  Of two-and-twenty or, by'r Lady, thirty.

Tranio. By'r Lady, I'll require my wager then,   35
  For, if you kiss so often and no kindness,
  I have lost my speculation. I'll allow ye –

---

22. *honesty*] decency; courtesy.

24. *sin-off'ring*] an offering in atonement for sin. (Biblical; refers to the betting of money.)

25. *daintily*] deftly.

26. *toil*] net.

leap it] leap over it.

27. *woodman*] hunter.

by] according to.

28. *equal*] all the same.

29. *what goes less?*] how about a smaller bet?

32. *affect*] love.

32–4. *Yet . . . thirty*] Still it may be the case that this son-of-a-bitch courtesy will require some twenty-two or thirty kisses.

35. *require my wager*] call in my bet.

36. *no kindness*] without encouragement.

37. *lost my speculation*] i.e., lost the money I bet.

Roland. Speak like a gamester now.
Tranio.   It may be, two.
Roland. Under a dozen, Tranio, there's no setting.
    You shall have forty shillings, wink at small faults.   40
    Say I take twenty; come, by all that's honest,
    I do it but to vex her.
Tranio.   I'll no by-blows.
    If you can love her, do. If ye can hate her,
    Or any else that loves ye –
Roland.   Prithee, Tranio –
Tranio. Why, farewell, twenty pound! 'Twill not undo me.   45
    You have my resolution.
Roland.   And your money –
    Which, since you are so stubborn, if I forfeit,
    Make me a jack-o'-Lent, and break my shins
    For untagged points and counters. I'll go with you.
    But if thou get'st a penny by the bargain –   50
    A parting kiss is lawful?
Tranio.   I allow it.
Roland. Knock out my brains with apples. Yet a bargain?
Tranio. I tell you, I'll no bargains. Win and wear it.
Roland. Thou art the strangest fellow.
Tranio.   That's all one.
Roland. Along, then. Twenty pound more, if thou dar'st,   55
    I give her not a good word.
Tranio.   Not a penny.   *Exeunt.*

---

38. *gamester*] gambler.
   two] two kisses.
39. *there's no setting*] the bet is off.
42. *I'll no by-blows*] I'll take no bets on the side. (By-blows are to the side, not direct hits.)
45. *undo*] bankrupt.
46. *You . . . resolution*] You know how my mind is made up.
48. *jack-o'-Lent*] figure of a man set up to be pelted.
49. *untagged points*] laces without the ornamental metal ends; hence, a worthless item.
   counters] disks used in lieu of currency, of no intrinsic value.
53. *Win . . . it*] i.e., Boast about it once you've won (proverbial).

4.4

         Enter PETRUCCIO, JAQUES, *and* PEDRO.

Petruccio. Prithee, entreat her come. I will not trouble her
    Above a word or two.   *Exit* PEDRO.
                    Ere I endure
    This life – and with a woman, and a vowed one
    To all the mischiefs she can lay upon me –
    I'll go to plough again and eat leek-porridge.   5
    Begging's a pleasure to't, not to be numbered.
    No, there be other countries, Jaques, for me,
    And other people, yea and other women,
    If I have need: 'here's money' – 'there's your ware'
    (Which is fair dealing). And the sun, they say,   10
    Shines as warm there as here, and till I have lost
    Either myself or her – I care not whether,
    Nor which first –
Jaques.   Will Your Worship hear me?
Petruccio. And utterly outworn the memory
    Of such a curse as this, none of my nation   15
    Shall ever know me more.
Jaques.   Out, alas, sir,
    What a strange way do you run?
Petruccio.   Any way,
    So I outrun this rascal.
Jaques.   Methinks now,
    If Your good Worship could but have the patience –
Petruccio. The patience! Why the patience?
Jaques.   Why, I'll tell you.   20

    4.4] Petruccio and Maria's house.

    2. *Above*] with more than.

    3. *a vowed one*] one who is committed.

    5. *go to plough*] i.e., till the soil, work as a ploughman. (The 'again' implies
a humble background.)

    5. *leek-porridge*] a meal associated with peasants.

    6. *to't*] compared to it.

    not . . . numbered] incalculable.

    9. *ware*] merchandise (here, sexual).

    12. *whether*] which.

    18. *rascal*] (Maria).

Could you but have the patience –
Petruccio.   Well, the patience.
Jaques. To laugh at all she does or, when she rails,
    To have a drum beaten o'th' top o'th' house,
    To give the neighbours warning of her 'larum,
    As I do when my wife rebels –
Petruccio.   *Thy* wife?   25
    Thy wife's a pigeon to her, a mere slumber;
    The dead of night's not stiller.
Jaques.   Nor an iron mill.
Petruccio. But thy wife is certain.
Jaques.   That's false doctrine.
    You never read yet of a certain woman.
Petruccio. Thou know'st her way.
Jaques.   I should do, I am sure.   30
    I have ridden it night and day, this twenty year.
Petruccio. But mine is such a drench of balderdash,
    Such a strange carded cunningness, the rainbow,
    When she hangs bent in heaven, sheds not her colours
    Quicker, and more, than this deceitful woman   35
    Weaves in her dyes of wickedness.

            Enter PEDRO.

                    What says she?
Pedro. Nay, not a word, sir. But she pointed to me,
    As though she meant to follow. Pray, sir, bear it
    Easy as you may. I need not teach Your Worship
    The best man hath his crosses. We are all mortal.   40
Petruccio. [*To Jaques*] What ails the fellow?
Pedro.   And no doubt she may, sir –

---

24. *'larum*] call to arms.
28. *certain*] constant; faithful.
30. *way*] ways.
31. *ridden it*] (Jaques plays on 'way' to the house and 'way' into her body.)
32. *drench of balderdash*] dose of a strange concoction.
33. *carded*] adulterated by mixing. (From the card used to remove impurities from wool before spinning.)
34. *she hangs bent*] (The Roman deity of the rainbow was Iris, a goddess; describing her as 'bent' sexualizes the image.)
39. *Easy*] as easily as.
40. *The best man*] even the most virtuous man (Jesus?).
    crosses] burdens.

Petruccio. What may she? Or what does she? Or what is she?
  Speak and be hanged!
Pedro.   She's mad, sir.
Petruccio.   [God] continue it.
Pedro. Amen, if't be his pleasure.
Petruccio.   How mad is she?
Pedro. As mad as heart can wish, sir. She has dressed herself   45
  (Saving Your Worship's reverence) just i'th' cut
  Of one of those that multiply i'th' suburbs
  For single money, and as dirtily.
  If any speak to her, first she whistles,
  And then begins her compass with her fingers,   50
  And points to what she would have.
Petruccio.   What new way's this?
Pedro. There came in master Sophocles –
Petruccio.   And what
  Did master Sophocles, when he came in? –
  Get my trunks ready, sirrah; I'll be gone straight.

                    Enter SOPHOCLES.

Pedro. He's here to tell you. –   55
    She's horn-mad, Jaques.   [*Exeunt* PEDRO *and* JAQUES.]
Sophocles.   Call ye this a woman?
Petruccio. Yes, sir, she is a woman.
Sophocles.   Sir, I doubt it.
Petruccio. I had thought you had made experience.
Sophocles.   Yes, I did so,
  And almost with my life.
Petruccio.   You rid too fast, sir.
Sophocles. Pray, be not you mistaken. By this light,   60
  Your wife is chaste and honest as a virgin,

---

46. *Saving . . . reverence*] begging your pardon, sir.
i'th' cut] in the fashion.
47. *those . . . suburbs*] prostitutes, who proliferated outside the city limits.
48. *single money*] small change.
50. *begins her compass*] draws a circle.
53. *came in*] (With sexual innuendo.)
56. *horn-mad*] mad as a horned animal ready to charge. (Also alluding to the cuckold's horns.)
58. *made experience*] tried it out (by having sex with her).
59. *rid*] rode.

For anything I know. 'Tis true, she gave me
    A ring.
Petruccio.   For rutting.
Sophocles.   You are much deceived still.
    ['Od's me], I never kissed her since, and now
    Coming in visitation like a friend –   65
    I think she is mad, sir – suddenly she started
    And snatched the ring away and drew her knife out,
    To what intent I know not.
Petruccio.   Is this certain?
Sophocles. As I am here, sir.
Petruccio.   I believe you honest –
    And, pray, continue so.
Sophocles.   She comes.

                 Enter MARIA.

Petruccio.   Now, damsel,   70
    What will your beauty do, if I forsake you?
                       [*She makes signs.*]
    Do you deal by signs and tokens? As I guess, then,
    You'll walk abroad this summer and catch captains,
    Or hire a piece of holy ground i'th' suburbs
    And keep a nest of nuns?
Sophocles.   Oh, do not stir her!   75
    You see in what a case she is.
Petruccio.   She is dogged,
    And in a beastly case, I am sure. I'll make her,
    If she have any tongue, yet tattle. Sophocles,
    Prithee, observe this woman seriously
    And eye her well, and (when thou hast done) but tell
      me –   80

---

63. *rutting*] fornicating. (The ring represents her vagina.)

64. *'Od's me*] (An oath, beginning with a changed form of *God's*.)

66. *started*] recoiled.

71.1. makes signs] gestures as if using sign-language.

72. *tokens*] symbols.

73. *captains*] i.e., whoremongers.

74–5. *hire . . . nuns*] 'nunnery' was a slang term for 'brothel'; both institutions were associated with the suburbs.

75. *stir*] upset.

76. *dogged*] dog-like; 'a bitch'.

80. *but*] simply.

For thou hast understanding – in what case
My sense was, when I chose this thing.
Sophocles.   I'll tell you,
     I have seen a sweeter –
Petruccio.   A hundred times, cry oysters.
     There's a poor beggar wench about Blackfriars
     Runs on her breech, may be an empress to her.   85
Sophocles. Nay, now you are too bitter.
Petruccio.   Never a whit, sir. –
     I'll tell thee, woman, for now I have day to see thee
     And all my wits about me, and I'll speak
     Not out of passion neither – leave your mumping;
     I know you're well enough. [*Aside*] Now would I give   90
     A million but to vex her. [*To Maria*] When I chose thee
     To make a bedfellow, I took more trouble
     Than twenty terms can come to: such a cause
     Of such a title, and so everlasting
     That Adam's genealogy may be ended   95
     Ere any law find thee. I took a leprosy;
     Nay, worse, the plague; nay, worse yet, a possession,
     And had the devil with thee, if not more;
     And yet worse, was a beast, and like a beast
     Had my reward, a jade to fling my fortunes –   100
     For who that had but reason to distinguish
     The light from darkness, wine from water, hunger
     From full satiety, and fox from fern-bush,

---

83. *cry oysters*] (Women oyster-sellers were stereotypically loud and ill-smelling.)

84. *Blackfriars*] a London district (this may also be a stab at a rival company housed in Blackfriars theatre).

85. *Runs . . . breech*] i.e., suffers from bladder incontinence.

to] compared to.

86. *Never a whit*] Not at all.

89. *mumping*] making faces.

92. *took*] took on.

93. *terms*] court sessions.

93–6. *such . . . thee*] Adam's genealogy (i.e. the human race) will come to an end before the case against you can be resolved in law.

98. *had . . . more*] had one devil in you, if not more.

100. *fling*] fling away.

101. *who*] who is there.

That would have married thee?
Sophocles.   She is not so ill.
Petruccio. She's worse than I dare think of. She's so lewd   105
    No court is strong enough to bear her cause.
    She hath neither manners, honesty, behaviour,
    Wifehood, nor womanhood, nor any mortal
    Can force me think she had a mother. No,
    I do believe her steadfastly and know her   110
    To be a woman-wolf by transmigration.
    Her first form was a ferret's underground;
    She kills the memories of men. [*Aside*] Not yet?
Sophocles. Do you think she's sensible of this?
Petruccio.   I care not.
    Be what she will, the pleasure I take in her   115
    Thus I blow off. The care I took to love her,
    Like this point, I untie, and thus I loose it.
    The husband I am to her, thus I sever.
    [*To Maria*] My vanity, farewell. Yet, for you have been
    So near me as to bear the name of wife,   120
    My unquenched charity shall tell you thus much:
    Though you deserve it well, you shall not beg.
    What I ordained your jointure, honestly
    You shall have settled on you, and half my house.
    The other half shall be employed in prayers –   125
    That meritorious charge I'll be at also –
    Yet to confirm ye Christian. Your apparel,

---

104. *ill*] bad.
105. *lewd*] indecent.
106. *bear her cause*] entertain her case.
111. *transmigration*] (Referring to the heretical belief in the transmigration or reincarnation of the soul.)
113. *She . . . men*] i.e., she blackens their reputations for all time.
Not yet?] This hasn't provoked her yet?
114. *sensible*] aware.
116. *blow off*] throw to the winds.
117. *point*] lace. (Petruccio gestures as he unties his lace.)
119. *My vanity*] (Maria).
for] because.
123. *jointure*] marriage settlement.
124. *settled on you*] legally bequeathed to you.
house] estate.
126. *charge*] expense.
be at] undertake.

And what belongs to build up such a folly,
Keep, I beseech ye; it infects our uses.
And now I am for travel.
Maria.   Now I love ye.   130
And, now I see ye are a man, I'll talk to ye –
And I forgive your bitterness.
Sophocles. [*To Petruccio*]   How now, man?
Petruccio. O Pliny, if thou wilt be ever famous,
Make but this woman all thy wonders.
Maria.   Sure, sir,
You have hit upon a happy course, a blessèd,   135
And what will make you virtuous.
Petruccio. [*Aside*]   She'll ship me.
Maria. A way of understanding I long wished for.
And, now 'tis come, take heed you fly not back, sir.
Methinks you look a new man to me now,
A man of excellence, and now I see   140
Some great design set in ye. You may think now –
And so may most that know me – 'twere my part
Weakly to weep your loss, and to resist ye,
Nay, hang about your neck and, like a dotard,
Urge my strong tie upon ye. But I love ye,   145
And all the world shall know it, beyond woman,
And more prefer the honour of your country

---

129. *uses*] endeavours.
130. *for*] prepared for.
131. *now*] now that.
133. *Pliny*] Pliny the Elder (23–79 CE), author of a classical encyclopedia of natural science containing many monsters and wonders.
135. *course*] plan.
136. *ship me*] send me off.
137. *understanding*] wisdom.
138. *fly not back*] don't fly back.
141. *design*] providential plan; fate.
142. *most . . . me*] (Probably metatheatrical: most spectators familiar with my previous roles.)
part] role.
143. *weep*] mourn.
resist ye] argue with you.
144. *dotard*] one who foolishly dotes.
145. *Urge . . . ye*] i.e., plead on the basis of my (marital) bond to you.
146. *beyond woman*] more than any other woman could.

(Which chiefly you are born for, and may perfect),
The uses you may make of other nations,
The ripening of your knowledge, conversation,   150
The full ability and strength of judgement,
Than any private love or wanton kisses.
Go, worthy man, and bring home understanding.
Sophocles. [*Aside*] This were an excellent woman to breed
    schoolmen.
Maria. For, if the merchant through unknown seas plough   155
    To get his wealth, then, dear sir, what must you
    To gather wisdom? Go, and go alone,
    Only your noble mind for your companion.
    And, if a woman may win credit with you,
    Go far – too far you cannot; still the farther,   160
    The more experience finds you – and go sparing.
    One meal a week will serve you, and one suit,
    Through all your travels – for you'll find it certain,
    The poorer and the baser ye appear,
    The more you look through still.
Petruccio. [*To Sophocles*]   Dost hear her?
Sophocles.   Yes.   165
Petruccio. What would this woman do, if she were suffered,
    Upon a new religion?
Sophocles.   Make us pagans.
    I wonder that she writes not.
Maria. [*To Petruccio*]   Then, when time
    And fullness of occasion have new-made you
    And squared you from a sot into a senior   170

---

148. *perfect*] (stressed on the first syllable).

154. *schoolmen*] (1) scholars; (2) sophists, double-talkers.

159. *win credit with*] persuade.

160. *too . . . cannot*] i.e., no distance would be far enough.

161. *finds*] comes to.
go sparing] i.e., travel cheaply.

164. *The . . . still*] (1) the better you perceive past the surfaces of things; (2) the more your true worth shines through your poor appearance; (3) the more you look like yourself (i.e. base, poor).

166–7. *suffered . . . religion*] permitted to advocate a new religion.

168. *I . . . not*] I wonder that she doesn't turn to writing sermons and treatises. (A dig at women writers.)

169. *occasion*] opportunity.

170. *squared . . . senior*] transformed you from a fool into (1) an old man; (2) a church elder; (3) an Italian gentleman, a *signore.*

Or, nearer, from a jade into a courser,
Come home an agèd man, as did Ulysses,
And I, your glad Penelope –
Petruccio.   That must have
As many lovers as I languages,
And what she does with one i'th' day, i'th' night   175
Undo it with another.
Maria.   Much that way, sir.
For in your absence it must be my honour,
That that must make me spoken of hereafter,
To have temptations (and no little ones)
Daily and hourly offered me (and strongly),   180
Almost believed against me, to set off
The faith and loyalty of her that loves ye.
Petruccio. [*Aside to Sophocles*] What should I do?
Sophocles. [*Aside to Petruccio*] Why, by my troth, I would travel.
Did not you mean so?
Petruccio. [*Aside to Sophocles*] Alas, no! nothing less, man.
I did it but to try her. She's the devil –   185
And now I find it, for she drives me. I must go.
[*Calling*] Are my trunks down there, and my horses
ready?
Maria. Sir, for your house, and if you please to trust me
With that you leave behind –
Petruccio. [*Calling*]   Bring down the money!

---

171. *nearer*] rather.
   courser] race-horse.
172. *Ulysses*] hero of Homer's *Odyssey*, whose wife, Penelope, remained faithful throughout his twenty-year travels, rebuffing many suitors with the excuse of weaving she needed to finish (which she undid each night).
175–6. *does . . . Undo*] (Petruccio sexualizes Penelope's weaving, suggesting that she wasn't in fact chaste.)
176. *Much that way*] Something like that.
178. *That that*] that which.
181. *set off*] highlight; show to advantage.
184. *nothing less*] anything but.
185–6. *devil . . . me*] (Alluding to the proverb 'He must needs go that the devil drives'.)
188. *for*] as for.
189. *that*] that which.

Maria. As I am able, and to my poor fortunes,   190
    I'll govern as a widow. I shall long
    To hear of your well-doing and your profit,
    And when I hear not from you once a quarter
    I'll wish you in the Indies or Cataia;
    Those are the climes must make you.
Petruccio.   How's the wind? –   195
    [*Aside*] She'll wish me out o'th' world anon.
Maria.   For France
    'Tis very fair. Get you aboard tonight, sir,
    And lose no time. You know the tide stays no man.
    I have cold meats ready for you.
Petruccio.   Fare thee well.
    Thou hast fooled me out o'th' kingdom with a vengeance,   200
    And thou canst fool me in again.
Maria.   Not I, sir.
    I love you better. Take your time and pleasure.
    I'll see you horsed.
Petruccio.   I think thou wouldst see me hanged too,
    Were I but half as willing.
Maria.   Anything
    That you think well of, I dare look upon.   205
Petruccio. You'll bear me to the land's end, Sophocles,
    And other o' my friends, I hope?
Maria.   Nev'r doubt, sir.
    Ye cannot want companions for your good.
    I am sure you'll kiss me ere I go. I have business,
    And stay long here I must not.
Petruccio.   Get thee going –   210
    For if thou tarriest but another dialogue,
    I'll kick thee to thy chamber.

---

190. *to*] to the extent of.
192. *profit*] prospering.
194. *Cataia*] China (Cathay).
195. *must make you*] that must profit you.
196–7. *For . . . fair*] The wind is favourable for sailing to France.
198. *stays*] waits for.
200. *fooled*] tricked.
203. *horsed*] (1) on horse-back; (2) hoisted up in order to be flogged.
206. *bear . . . end*] bring me to the shore.
211. *tarriest . . . dialogue*] linger to talk more.

Maria.   Fare ye well, sir.
  And bear yourself (I do beseech ye once more),
  Since you have undertaken doing wisely,
  Manly and worthily; 'tis for my credit.   215
  And for those flying fames here of your follies,
  Your gambols, and ill breeding of your youth,
  For which I understand you take this travel –
  Nothing should make me leave you else – I'll deal
  So like a wife that loves your reputation   220
  And the most large addition of your credit,
  That those shall die. If ye want lemon-water,
  Or anything to take the edge o'th' sea off,
  Pray, speak, and be provided.
Petruccio.   Now the devil,
  That was your first good master, show'r his blessing   225
  Upon ye all! Into whose custody –
Maria. I do commit your reformation.
  And so I leave you to your *stilo novo.*   *Exit.*
Petruccio. I will go. Yet I will not. Once more, Sophocles,
  I'll put her to the test.
Sophocles.   You had better go.   230
Petruccio. I will go, then. Let's seek my father out
  And all my friends, to see me fair aboard.
  Then, women, if there be a storm at sea
  Worse than your tongues can make, and waves more
    broken
  Than your dissembling faiths are, let me feel   235
  Nothing but tempests, till they crack my keel!   *Exeunt.*

---

213. *beseech ye*] ask of you.

215. *credit*] honour.

216. *for . . fames*] as for those fleeting rumours.

217. *gambols*] frolics; merry-making.

223. *the edge . . . sea*] sea-sickness. (Ironically, it was not then generally known that citric acid also warded off scurvy.)

226–7. *Into . . . reformation*] (Parody of a liturgical phrase.)

228. stilo novo] (1) 'new style' (Italian); (2) a phrase used in dates on letters from continental Europe, which had adopted the new calendar in 1582 (not used in England until the eighteenth century).

231. *father*] father-in-law.

233. *women*] (the women in the audience: compare 'gentlemen' at 3.3.147).

Act 5

Enter PETRONIUS *and* BIANCA, *with four papers.*

Bianca. Now whether I deserve that blame you gave me,
    Let all the world discern, sir.
Petronius.   If this motion –
    I mean, this fair repentance of my daughter –
    Spring from your good persuasion, as it seems so,
    I must confess I have spoke too boldly of you,   5
    And I repent.
Bianca.   The first touch was her own,
    Taken no doubt from disobeying you;
    The second I put to her, when I told her
    How good and gentle yet, with free contrition,
    Again you might be purchased. Loving woman!   10
    She heard me, and (I thank her) thought me worthy
    Observing in this point. Yet all my counsel
    And comfort in this case could not so heal her
    But that grief got his share too, and she sickened.
Petronius. I am sorry she's so ill, yet glad her sickness   15
    Has got so good a ground.

5.1] Petronius's house.

5.1.0.1 four papers] Roland and Livia have arranged to sign a contract
(in duplicate) annulling their verbal engagement. Unbeknownst to Roland,
Bianca has drafted a legally binding marriage pre-contract (common at the
time). The first pair of duplicates Livia uses as dummies to fool Petronius
and Moroso, who read one pair of papers and then sign the other pair. In
the darkened bedchamber, she will substitute the second set of papers (see
5.1.120). The old men are thus duped into endorsing the young couple's
marriage.

6. *touch*] touch of remorse.

8. *put to*] inspired in.

10. *purchased*] won over.

12. *Observing*] heeding.

16. *ground*] moral cause.

Enter MOROSO.

Bianca. Here comes Moroso.
Petronius. [*To Moroso*] Oh, you are very welcome.
    Now you shall know your happiness.
Moroso.   I am glad on't.
    What makes this lady here?
Bianca.   A dish for you, sir,   20
    You'll thank me for hereafter.
Petronius.   True, Moroso.
    Go, get you in, and see your mistress.
Bianca. [*To Moroso*]   She is sick, sir,
    But you may kiss her whole.
Moroso.   How!
Bianca.   Comfort her.
Moroso. Why am I sent for, sir?
Petronius.   Will you in and see?
Bianca. May be she needs confession.
Moroso.   By St Mary,   25
    She shall have absolution then, and penance;
    But not above her carriage.
Petronius.   Get you in, fool.

                             Exit MOROSO.

Enter ROLAND *and* TRANIO.

Bianca. Here comes the other, too.
Petronius.   Now, Tranio! –
    [*To Roland*] Good e'en to you too, and you're welcome.
Roland.   Thank you.
Petronius. I have a certain daughter –
Roland.   Would you had, sir!   30

---

19. *on't*] of it.

20. *makes*] does.

23. *kiss her whole*] kiss her back to health. (But the homophone of 'hole' makes for an obscene joke at Moroso's expense.)

27. *carriage*] (1) conduct, i.e., what her behaviour warrants; (2) ability to bear (with an insinuation about the bearing of a man's sexual weight).

29. *Good e'en*] (Contraction for 'God give you good evening'.)

30. *Would you had*] (Roland quibbles on the sense of 'certain' as constant, faithful.)

Petronius. No doubt you know her well.
Roland.   Nor never shall, sir.
    She is a woman, and the ways into her
    Are like the finding of a certain path
    After a deep-fall'n snow.
Petronius.   Well, that's by the by still.
    This daughter that I tell you of is fall'n   35
    A little crop-sick with the dangerous surfeit
    She took of your affection.
Roland.   Mine, sir?
Petronius. I think 'twere well you would see her.
Roland.   If you please, sir.
    I am not squeamish of my visitation.
Petronius. But this I'll tell you: she is altered much.   40
    You'll find her now another Livia.
Roland. I had enough o'th' old, sir.
Petronius.   No more fool
    To look gay babies in your eyes, young Roland,
    And hang about your pretty neck –
Roland.   I am glad on't,
    And thank my fates I have scaped such executions.   45
Petronius. And buss you till you blush again.
Roland.   That's hard, sir.
    She must kiss shamefully ere I blush at it;
    I never was so boyish. Well, what follows?
Petronius. She's mine now, as I please to settle her,
    At my command, and where I please to plant her;   50
    Only she would take a kind of farewell of ye,
    And give you back a wand'ring vow or two

---

31. *Nor never shall*] No, and I never will.

32. *ways into her*] ways of knowing her. (With sexual innuendo.)

34. *by-the-by*] beside the point.

36. *crop-sick*] sick to the stomach. (The crop is the intestinal tract.)

39. *of*] about.

42–3. *No . . . eyes*] She is no longer the sort of fool to gaze lovingly into your eyes. (The 'babies' are the small reflections of the viewer in the eyes of the beloved.)

45. *executions*] hard fates. (Punning on 'hanging'.)

46. *buss*] kiss.

hard] hard to do.

49. *settle*] place.

You left in pawn – and two or three slight oaths
She lent you too, she looks for.

Roland.   She shall have 'em
With all my heart, sir; and, if you like it better,   55
A free release in writing.

Petronius.   That's the matter.
And you from her shall have another, Roland,
And then turn tail to tail, and peace be with you.

Roland. [Faith,] so be it. – Your twenty pound sweats, Tranio.

Tranio. 'Twill not undo me, Roland. Do your worst.   60

Roland. [*To Petronius*] Come, shall we see her, sir?

Bianca.   Whate'er she says
You must bear manly, Roland, for her sickness
Has made her somewhat teatish.

Roland.   Let her talk
Till her tongue ache, I care not. By this hand,
Thou hast a handsome face, wench, and a body   65
Daintily mounted.

> *Enter* LIVIA *sick, carried in a chair by* Servants,
> *and* MOROSO *by her.*

[*Aside*] Now do I feel a hundred
Running directly from me, as I pissed it.

Bianca. Pray, bear her softly. The least hurry, sir,
Puts her to much impatience.

Petronius.   How is't, daughter?

Livia. Oh, sick, very sick! Yet somewhat better,   70
Because this good man has forgiven me.
[*To Bianca*] Pray, set me higher. Oh, my head!

Bianca. [*Aside to Livia*]   Well done, wench.

---

56. *matter*] business at hand.
57. *another*] another release.
59. *Faith*] (A mild oath.)
Your . . . sweats] (Rowland is tempted to break his vow against loving her,
and hence lose the bet.)
63. *teatish*] cranky (like a newly-weaned or hungry infant).
67. *as*] as if.
68. *bear her softly*] i.e., treat her gently.
69. *Puts . . . impatience*] makes her fretful.
71. *good man*] (Moroso).

Livia. Father, and all good people that shall hear me,
    I have abused this man perniciously.
    Was never old man humbled so. I have scorned him   75
    And called him nasty names. I have spit at him,
    Flung candles' ends in's beard, and called him 'harrow',
    That must be drawn to all he does; contemned him,
    For methought then he was a beastly fellow –
    O God, my side! – a very beastly fellow;   80
    And gave it out his cassock was a barge-cloth
    Pawned to his predecessor by a sculler,
    The man yet extant. I gave him purging comfits
    At a great christening once,
    That spoiled his camlet breeches, and one night   85
    I strewed the stairs with peas, as he passed down,
    And the good gentleman – woe worth me for't! –
    Ev'n with his reverent head, this head of wisdom,
    Told two-and-twenty stairs, good and true,
    Missed not a step and, as we say, verbatim   90
    Fell to the bottom, broke his casting-bottle,
    Lost a fair toad-stone of some eighteen shillings,
    Jumbled his joints together, had two stools,
    And was translated. All this villainy
    Did I; I, Livia, I alone, untaught.   95

---

77. *in's*] in his.
harrow] a plough.
78. *all he does*] (including sex).
contemned] scorned.
80. *my side*] source of my feigned pain. (But also suggesting God's provision of a companion for Adam, by removing a rib from his side: Moroso reverses gender hierarchy, by being a 'beast' who is inferior to, only a small part of, a woman.)
81. *barge-cloth*] protective cover used on a barge.
82. *sculler*] menial labourer who rows a boat or barge for a living.
83. *purging comfits*] candied laxatives.
85. *camlet*] a fine fabric made with silk and Angora hair.
87. *woe . . . for't*] i.e., I deserve woe for it.
89. *Told*] (1) counted (while falling); (2) tolled.
90. *verbatim*] precisely.
91. *casting-bottle*] bottle for sprinkling perfumed water.
92. *toad-stone*] stone fabled to be found in a toad's head.
93. *stools*] bowel movements.
94. *translated*] carried out of his senses.

Moroso. And I, unasked, forgive it.

Livia.   Where's Bianca?

Bianca. Here, cousin.

Livia.   Give me drink.

Bianca. [*Giving her drink*]   There.

Livia.   Who's that?

Moroso.   Roland.

Livia. [*To Roland*] O my dissembler, you and I must part.
    Come nearer, sir.

Roland.   I am sorry for your sickness.

Livia. Be sorry for yourself, sir. You have wronged me,   100
    But I forgive ye. – Are the papers ready?

Bianca. I have 'em here. – Will't please you view 'em?

Petronius.   Yes.

Livia. Show 'em the young man too. I know he's willing
    To shift his sails too. 'Tis for his more advancement.
    Alas, we might have beggared one another.   105
    We are young both, and a world of children
    Might have been left behind to curse our follies.
    We had been undone, Bianca, had we married,
    Undone for ever. I confess I loved him –
    I care not who shall know it – most entirely,   110
    And once, upon my conscience, he loved me.
    But farewell that. We must be wiser, cousin.
    Love must not leave us to the world. Have ye done?

Roland. Yes, and am ready to subscribe.

Livia.   Pray, stay then.
    Give me the papers – and let me peruse 'em –   115
    And so much time as may afford a tear
    At our last parting.

Bianca. [*To the men*]   Pray, retire, and leave her.
    I'll call ye presently.

Petronius.   Come, gentlemen.

---

103. *Show 'em*] Show them to.

104. *shift his sails*] i.e., change his course.

   more] greater.

113. *leave . . . world*] i.e., leave us unprovided for, at the mercy of an indifferent world.

   done] finished reading the contract.

114, 122. *subscribe*] sign as witness(es).

The shower must fall.

Roland.   Would I had never seen her!

> *Exeunt all but Bianca and Livia.*

Bianca. Thou hast done bravely, wench.

Livia.   Pray [God] it prove so.   120

Bianca. There are the other papers. When they come,

   Begin you first, and let the rest subscribe

   Hard by your side. Give 'em as little light

   As drapers do their wares.

Livia.   Didst mark Moroso,

   In what an agony he was, and how he cried most   125

   When I abused him most?

Bianca.   That was but reason.

Livia. Oh, what a stinking thief it is!

   Though I was but to counterfeit, he made me

   Directly sick indeed. Thames Street to him

   Is a mere pomander.   130

Bianca. Let him be hanged.

Livia. Amen.

Bianca.   And sit you still,

   And once more to our business.

Livia.   Call 'em in.

   And if there be a pow'r that pities lovers,

   Help now, and hear my prayers!

> [BIANCA *goes to the door and opens it.*]

Enter PETRONIUS, ROLAND, TRANIO, [*and*] MOROSO.

Petronius. [*To Bianca*]   Is she ready?   135

Bianca. She has done her lamentations. Pray, go to her.

---

119. *shower*] tears.

120. *bravely*] excellently.

123. *Hard*] close.

123–4. *Give . . . wares*] i.e., Keep the room as dark as cloth merchants do when they are trying to sell bad merchandise.

126. *but reason*] only right.

127. *it*] (familiar pronoun for a child, i.e., Moroso).

128. *counterfeit*] fake it.

129–30. *Thames . . . pomander*] Thames Street, in comparison to him, is an absolute perfume bottle. (Thames Street was known for the smell of fish and tar.)

132. *sit you still*] stay in your invalid's chair.

Livia. Roland, come near me. And before you seal,
      Give me your hand. Take it again. Now kiss me.
      This is the last acquaintance we must have.
      I wish you ever happy. There's the paper.   140
Roland. Pray, stay a little.
Petronius. [*Aside to the others*] Let me never live more,
      But I do begin to pity this young fellow.
      How heartily he weeps!
Bianca. [*To Roland*]   There's pen and ink, sir.
Livia. [*To Roland*] Ev'n here, I pray you. 'Tis a little emblem
      How near you have been to me.
Roland. [*Signing*]   There.
Bianca. [*To Petronius and Moroso*]   Your hands too,   145
      As witnesses.
Petronius.   By any means. [*To Moroso*] To th' book, son.
Moroso. With all my heart.
                    [*Petronius and Moroso sign the first deed.*]
Bianca. [*To Roland*]   You must deliver it.
Roland. There, Livia, and a better love light on thee!
      I can no more.
Bianca. [*To Petronius and Moroso*] To this you must be
          witness too.
Petronius. We will.
                    [*Petronius and Moroso sign the second deed.*]
Bianca.   Do you deliver it now.
Livia.   Pray, set me up. –   150
      There, Roland, all thy old love back, and may
      A new to come exceed mine, and be happy!
      I must no more.
Roland.   Farewell!
Livia.   A long farewell!
                              Exit ROLAND.

---

137. *seal*] sign, then authenticate the document with a wax seal.
141. *stay a little*] i.e., don't die yet.
144. *emblem*] symbol.
145. *near*] close; dear.
146. *book*] official document.
148. *a better . . . thee*] may you find more happiness in love with another.
149. *can*] can do.
151. *all . . . back*] I give you all your love back.

Bianca. Leave her, by any means, till this wild passion
    Be off her head.   155
    A day hence you may see her. 'Twill be better.
    She is now for little company.
Petronius.   Pray, tend her.
    I must to horse straight. [*To Moroso*] You must needs
        along too,
    To see my son aboard. Were but his wife
    As fit for pity as this wench, I were happy.   160
Bianca. Time must do that too. Fare ye well. [*To Moroso*]
    Tomorrow
    You shall receive a wife to quite your sorrow.   *Exeunt.*

5.2

    Enter JAQUES, PEDRO, *and* Porters *with a trunk and hampers.*

Jaques. Bring 'em away, sirs.
Pedro.   Must the great trunk go too?
Jaques. Yes, and the hampers. – Nay, be speedy, masters.
    He'll be at sea before us else.
Pedro.   Oh, Jaques,
    What a most blessèd turn hast thou –
Jaques.   I hope so.
Pedro. To have the sea between thee and this woman!   5
    Nothing can drown her tongue but a storm.
Jaques.   By your leave,
    We'll get us up to Paris with all speed;
    For (on my soul) as far as Amiens
    She'll carry blank. [*To porters*] Away to Lyon quay

---

158. *must . . . straight*] i.e., must be off right away.
must needs] must go.
159. *son*] son-in-law (Petruccio).
162. *quite*] requite, compensate for.

5.2] Petruccio and Maria's house.
4. *turn*] turn of luck.
8. *Amiens*] a city in France, north of Paris.
9. *carry blank*] fire a projectile on a level trajectory.
Lyon quay] the first wharf on the north side of the Thames; coming from
Blackfriars or Whitefriars, the closest dock for the big ships.

And ship 'em presently. We'll follow ye.   [*Exeunt* Porters.]   10
Pedro. Now could I wish her in that trunk.
Jaques.   God shield, man!
I had rather have a bear in't.
Pedro.   Yes, I'll tell ye,
For, in the passage, if a tempest take ye,
As many do, and you lie beating for it,
Then, if it pleased the fates, I would have the master,   15
Out of a careful providence, to cry
'Lighten the ship of all hands, or we perish!'
Then this for one, as best spared, should by all means
Overboard instantly.
Jaques.   O' that condition,
So we were certain to be rid of her,   20
I would wish her with us. But believe me, Pedro,
She would spoil the fishing on this coast for ever,
For none would keep her company but dog-fish,
As currish as herself, or porpoises
(Made to all fatal uses). The two Fish Streets,   25
Were she but once arrived among the whitings,
Would sing a woeful *misereri*, Pedro,
And mourn in poor john, till her memory
Were cast [ashore] again with a strong sea-breach.
She would make god Neptune and his fire-fork,   30

---

11. *God shield*] i.e., God forbid it.

13. *passage*] voyage.

14. *lie beating*] are sailing upwind.

18. *this*] the trunk (with Maria in it).

19. *Overboard*] be thrown overboard.

20. *So*] provided that.

23. *dog-fish*] small sharks.

24. *porpoises*] (Associated with storms; hence, bad luck to seamen.)

25. *The two Fish Streets*] Old Fish Street and New Fish Street in London; home of the fish markets.

26. *whitings*] a kind of fish (but perhaps also playing on the pale 'white' complexion stereotypically attributed to desirable women, and on the Whitefriars theatre).

27. misereri] have mercy on us.

28. *poor john*] a salted fish consumed by the lower classes.

29. *sea-breach*] surge.

30. *fire-fork*] trident.

And all his demigods and goddesses,
As weary of the Flemish channel, Pedro,
As ever boy was of the school. 'Tis certain,
If she but met him fair, and were well angered,
She would break his godhead.
Pedro.　　　　　　　　　　　Oh, her tongue, her tongue!　35
Jaques. Rather, her many tongues.
Pedro.　　　　　　　　　　Or rather, strange tongues.
Jaques. Her lying tongue,
Pedro.　　　　　　　Her lisping tongue,
Jaques.　　　　　　　　　　　Her long tongue,
Pedro. Her lawless tongue,
Jaques.　　　　　　　Her loud tongue,
Pedro.　　　　　　　　　　　And her liquorish –
Jaques. Many more tongues, and many stranger tongues
Than ever Babel had to tell his ruins,　　　　40
Were women raised withal; but never a true one.

Enter SOPHOCLES.

Sophocles. Home with your stuff again! The journey's ended.
Jaques. What does Your Worship mean?
Sophocles. Your master – Oh, Petruccio! Oh, poor fellows!
Pedro. Oh, Jaques, Jaques!
Sophocles.　　　　　　Oh, your master's dead!　　45
His body coming back. His wife, his devil,
The grief of her –
Jaques.　　　　　Has killed him?
Sophocles.　　　　　　　　Killed him, killed him.
Pedro. Is there no law to hang her?

---

32. *the Flemish channel*] the English Channel, separating England and Belgium.
　34. *him*] Neptune.
　fair] one-on-one.
　38. *liquorish*] lascivious.
　40. *Babel*] city and tower of which the attempted construction is described in Genesis (11:1–9). God punished the builders of the tower for their hubris by confusing their speech, so that they no longer spoke one tongue.
　41. *raised*] created, brought up (like a tower.)
　42. *ended*] cancelled.
　47. *of her*] caused by her.

Sophocles.   Get ye in
        And let her know her misery. I dare not,
        For fear impatience seize me, see her more.   50
        I must away again. Bid her for wifehood,
        For honesty – if she have any in her –
        Ev'n to avoid the shame that follows her,
        Cry if she can. *Your* weeping cannot mend it.
        The body will be here within this hour – so tell her –   55
        And all his friends to curse her. Farewell, fellows. *Exit.*
Pedro. Oh, Jaques, Jaques!
Jaques.   O my worthy master!
Pedro. O my most beastly mistress! Hang her!
Jaques.   Split her!
Pedro. Drown her directly!
Jaques.   Starve her!
Pedro.   [Shit] upon her!
Jaques. Stone her to death! May all she eat be eggs,   60
        Till she run kicking-mad for men!
Pedro.   And he,
        That man that gives her remedy, pray [God]
        He may ev'n *ipso facto* lose his faddings!
Jaques. Let's go discharge ourselves. And he that serves her,
        Or speaks a good word of her from this hour,   65
        A Sedgeley curse light on him – which is, Pedro,
        'The fiend ride through him booted and spurred, with a
        scythe at's back.'   *Exeunt.*

---

60. *eggs*] (Considered an aphrodisiac.)
61. *kicking-mad*] i.e., mad as a horse in heat.
63. ipso facto] by that fact.
    faddings] testicles.
64. *discharge ourselves*] (1) acquit ourselves of our obligations (as
Petruccio's servants); (2) vent our anger; (3) relieve ourselves sexually.
66. *Sedgeley curse*] a familiar curse named for a town ten miles north of
Birmingham. The curse yields multiple sexual connotations: the fiend, or
devil, will not only 'ride' the victim, but 'ride through him', i.e., penetrate
him anally, perhaps with the 'scythe', ambiguously placed at 'his' (either the
fiend's or the victim's) 'back'.

5.3

> *Enter* ROLAND [*with a paper,*] *and* TRANIO *stealing*
> *behind him.*

Roland. What a dull ass was I to let her go thus.
　　Upon my life, she loves me still. Well, paper,
　　Thou only monument of what I have had,
　　Thou all the love now left me, and now lost,
　　Let me yet kiss her hand, yet take my leave　　　　　5
　　Of what I must leave ever. Farewell, Livia!
　　O bitter words, I'll read ye once again,
　　And then forever study to forget ye.　　　[*He reads.*]
　　How's this? Let me look better on't. A contract?
　　[Good Lord,] a contract, sealed and ratified,　　　10
　　Her father's hand set to it, and Moroso's.
　　I do not dream, sure. Let me read again.　　[*He reads.*]
　　The same still. 'Tis a contract!
Tranio. [*Coming forward*]　　　　'Tis so, Roland,
　　And (by the virtue of the same) you pay me
　　A hundred pound tomorrow.
Roland.　　　　　　　　Art sure, Tranio,　　　15
　　We are both alive now?
Tranio.　　　　　　　Wonder not: ye have lost.
Roland. If this be true, I grant it.
Tranio.　　　　　　　　'Tis most certain.
　　There's a ring for you too. You know it?
　　　　　　　　　　[*Tranio gives Roland a ring.*]
Roland.　　　　　　　　　Yes.
Tranio. When shall I have my money?
Roland.　　　　　　　　Stay ye, stay.
　　When shall I marry her?
Tranio.　　　　　　Tonight.
Roland.　　　　　　　　Take heed now　　　20

5.3] Somewhere in London.
5. *hand*] handwriting.
8. *study*] strive; make an effort.
9. *contract*] marriage contract.
11. *Her . . . it*] signed by her father.
15. *Art*] Are you.
19. *Stay ye*] i.e., Hold on; wait a minute.

You do not trifle with me. If you do,
You'll find more payment than your money comes to.
Come, swear – I know I am a man, and find
I may deceive myself – swear faithfully,
Swear me directly: am I Roland?
Tranio.   Yes.   25
Roland. Am I awake?
Tranio.   Ye are.
Roland.   Am I in health?
Tranio. As far as I conceive.
Roland.   Was I with Livia?
Tranio. You were, and had this contract.
Roland.   And shall I enjoy her?
Tranio. Yes, if ye dare.
Roland.   Swear to all this.
Tranio.   I will.
Roland. As thou art honest, as thou hast a conscience,   30
    As that may wring thee if thou li'st: all these
    To be no vision, but a truth, and serious?
Tranio. Then by my honesty and faith and conscience,
    All this is certain.
Roland.   Let's remove our places.   [*They do so.*]
    Swear it again.
Tranio.   I swear, by [God], 'tis true.   35
Roland. I have lost then, and [God] knows I am glad on't.
    Let's go – and tell me all, and tell me how,
    For yet I am a pagan in it.
Tranio.   I have a priest too,
    And all shall come as even as two testers.   *Exeunt.*

---

22. *payment*] punishment.
31. *wring*] torment.
   li'st] tell a lie, liest.
34. *remove*] switch. (The line parodies *Hamlet*, 1.5.156–65, when Hamlet
and his friends move about on account of the ghost's calling from under the
stage.)
38. *a pagan in it*] i.e., unbelieving.
39. *testers*] coins worth six pence.

5.4

        Enter PETRONIUS, SOPHOCLES, MOROSO, [*with*]
          PETRUCCIO *in a coffin* carried *by* Servants.

Petronius. Set down the body, and one call her out.
                [*A servant goes to the door.*]

        Enter MARIA *in black,* JAQUES, [*and*] PEDRO.

You are welcome to the last cast of your fortunes.
There lies your husband, there your loving husband,
There he that was Petruccio, too good for ye.
Your stubborn and unworthy way has killed him   5
Ere he could reach the sea. If ye can weep,
Now ye have cause, begin, and after death
Do something yet to th' world, to think ye honest.
                [*Maria weeps.*]
So many tears had saved him, shed in time.
And as they are – so a good mind go with 'em –   10
Yet they may move compassion.
Maria.   Pray ye all, hear me
And judge me as I am, not as you covet,
For that would make me yet more miserable.
'Tis true, I have cause to grieve, a mighty cause,
And truly and unfeignedly I weep it.   15
Sophocles. I see there's some good nature yet left in her.
Maria. But what's the cause? Mistake me not. Not this man,
As he is dead, I weep for – heaven defend it!
I never was so childish – but his life,
His poor unmanly wretched foolish life,   20
Is that my full eyes pity. There's my mourning.

5.4] In front of Petruccio and Maria's house.
2. *cast*] throw of the dice.
8. *to think*] to let them think.
9. *had*] would have.
10. *so . . . 'em*] as long as good thoughts go with them.
12. *covet*] are inclined to think.
18. *defend*] forbid.
21. *Is that*] is that which.
  full] tear-filled.

Petronius. Dost thou not shame?
Maria.   I do, and even to water,
　　To think what this man was, to think how simple,
　　How far below a man, how far from reason,
　　From common understanding and all gentry,   25
　　While he was living here, he walked amongst us.
　　He had a happy turn; he died. I'll tell ye,
　　These are the wants I weep for, not his person.
　　The memory of this man, had he lived
　　But two years longer, had begot more follies   30
　　Than wealthy autumn flies. But let him rest –
　　He was a fool, and farewell! – not pitied
　　(I mean, in way of life or action)
　　By any understanding man that's honest,
　　But only in's posterity, which I,   35
　　Out of the fear his ruins might outlive him
　　In some bad issue, like a careful woman,
　　Like one indeed born only to preserve him,
　　Denied him means to raise.
　　　　　　　　　　　　Petruccio rises out of the coffin.
Petruccio.   Unbutton me!
　　[God wot], I die indeed else. O Maria,   40
　　Oh, my unhappiness, my misery!
Petronius. [*To Maria*] Go to him, whore! [God's my judge],
　　　　if he perish,

---

22. *Dost . . . shame?*] Are you not ashamed?
water] tears.
23. *simple*] foolish.
25. *gentry*] gentility.
27. *happy turn*] stroke of good luck.
28. *wants*] losses.
31. *wealthy autumn flies*] (A rich harvest in autumn would allow insects to flourish.)
35. *in's*] in his.
36. *his ruins*] i.e., the results of his poor behaviour.
37. *issue*] child he fathered. (Maria's point is that she did Petruccio a favor by not giving him the opportunity to have children with her.)
39. *Unbutton me!*] (A parody of King Lear's dying request, 'Pray you, undo this button' [5.2.285]; the utterance expresses a sense of being smothered or crushed inside.)
40. *wot*] knows.
42. *God's my judge*] As God is my judge. (A strong oath.)

I'll see thee hanged myself.

                [Petruccio comes out of the coffin.]

Petruccio.   Why, why, Maria –

Maria. I have done my worst, and have my end. Forgive me.

   From this hour make me what you please. I have tamed

     ye,   45

   And now am vowed your servant. Look not strangely,

   Nor fear what I say to you. Dare you kiss me?

   Thus I begin my new love.   *[They kiss.]*

Petruccio.   Once again.

Maria. With all my heart, sir.   *[They kiss.]*

Petruccio.   Once again, Maria.

                          [They kiss.]

   Oh, gentlemen, I know not where I am.   50

Sophocles. Get ye to bed then; there you'll quickly know, sir.

Petruccio. *[To Maria]* Never no more your old tricks?

Maria.   Never, sir.

Petruccio. You shall not need, for (as I have a faith)

   No cause shall give occasion.

Maria.   As I am honest

   And as I am a maid yet, all my life   55

   From this hour, since ye make so free profession,

   I dedicate in service to your pleasure.

Sophocles. Ay, marry, this goes roundly off.

Petruccio.   Go, Jaques,

   Get all the best meat may be bought for money,

   And let the hogsheads blood.   *[Exit* JAQUES.]

                  I am born again.   60

   Well, little England, when I see a husband

   Of any other nation stern or jealous,

---

44. *have my end*] am done.

53. *have a faith*] i.e., am a Christian.

54. *No . . . occasion*] i.e., I will not give you reason to.

honest] chaste.

58. *goes roundly off*] i.e., is a fair conclusion.

60. *let . . . blood*] i.e., open the beer kegs (literally, 'bleed' the kegs; open their vein).

61. *little England*] (1) Maria, as a diminutive embodiment of England; (2) the English nation: affectionate self-characterization, contrasting England with European superpowers like Spain and France (and 'Great Britain'). Petruccio's Italian origins in *Shrew* make this a compliment from a foreigner.

I'll wish him but a woman of thy breeding,
And if he have not butter to his bread
Till his teeth bleed, I'll never trust my travel.   65

Enter ROLAND, LIVIA, BIANCA, *and* TRANIO,
as from marriage.

Petronius. What have we here?
Roland.   Another morris, sir,
   That you must pipe to.
Tranio. [*To Petronius*]   A poor married couple
   Desire an offering, sir.
Bianca. [*To Petronius*]   Never frown at it.
   You cannot mend it now. There's your own hand –
   And yours, Moroso – to confirm the bargain.   70
                              [*She shows them papers.*]
Petronius. My hand?
Moroso.   Or mine?
Bianca.   You'll find it so.
Petronius.   A trick,
   By [God], a trick!
Bianca.   Yes, sir, we tricked ye.
Livia.   Father –
Petronius. Hast thou lain with him? Speak.
Livia.   Yes, truly, sir.
Petronius. And hast thou done the deed, boy?
Roland.   I have done, sir,
   That that will serve the turn, I think.
Petruccio.   A match, then.   75
   I'll be the maker-up of this. – Moroso,
   There's now no remedy, you see. Be willing,
   For (be or be not) he must have the wench.

---

63. *wish him*] wish for him.
   thy] Maria's (or England's).
66. *morris*] country dance.
68. *offering*] peace offering; dowry.
69. *hand*] signature.
   75. *serve the turn*] i.e., 'do the job'. (Rowland's and Livia's consummation
of their clandestine marriage makes it less vulnerable to legal contestation
by her father.)
76. *maker-up*] peace-maker.

Moroso. Since I am overreached, let's in to dinner,
    And (if I can) I'll drink't away.
Tranio.   That's well said.   80
Petronius. [*To Roland*] Well, sirrah, you have played a trick.
        Look to't,
    And let me be a grandsire within's twelvemonth
    Or, by this hand, I'll curtail half your fortunes.
Roland. There shall not want *my* labour, sir. – Your money
    Here's one has undertaken.
Tranio.   Well, I'll trust her,   85
    And glad I have so good a pawn.
Roland.   I'll watch ye.
Petruccio. Let's in, and drink of all hands, and be jovial.
    I have my colt again, and now she carries. –
    And gentlemen, whoever marries next,
    Let him be sure he keep him to his text.   90

                    Exeunt [*all but* MARIA].

Epilogue [*spoken by Maria*]
        The tamer's tamed – but so, as nor the men
        Can find one just cause to complain of, when
        They fitly do consider, in their lives
        They should not reign as tyrants o'er their wives;

---

79. *overreached*] outdone; out-smarted.
81. *Look to't*] See to the matter.
82. *within's*] within this.
83. *curtail*] cut off.
fortunes] dowry.
84. *my labour*] i.e., male sexual labour, distinguished from the labour of childbirth, with Livia.
84–5. *Your . . . undertaken*] Here's one (Livia) who has undertaken to pay the money I owe you (with a sexual pun on lie 'under' and 'take'.)
86. *pawn*] (He pretends that Livia is an object given to a pawnbroker as security on a loan – thus provoking Roland's jealous or mock-jealous reply.)
87. *drink . . . hands*] i.e., drinks all around.
90. *keep . . . text*] i.e., go by the book; follow the rules. (Perhaps referring to the text of the play itself.)
90.2. spoken by Maria] (Not specified in the 1647 text, but revivals of the play since 1660 have always given the last speech to Maria, and this was probably theatrical practice from the beginning.)
91. *nor*] neither.
93. *consider*] consider that.

Nor can the women from this precedent   95
Insult or triumph, it being aptly meant
To teach both sexes due equality
And, as they stand bound, to love mutually.
If this effect, arising from a cause
Well laid and grounded, may deserve applause,   100
We something more than hope our honest ends
Will keep the men, and women too, our friends.

---

96. *Insult or triumph*] vaunt proudly or boast.
98. *stand bound*] are obligated.
101–2.] We have high hopes that our honest efforts will win over both the men and the women in the audience.

Appendix: Additional Passages

After 1.3.11 [The omission of this short speech contributes to a general reduction of the Moroso subplot.]

Tranio. A good tough train would break thee all to pieces.
    Thou hast not breath enough to say thy prayers.

2.0 [This scene originally began Act 2, and was followed by what our edition – and the manuscript – identifies as 2.1. Like all the passages in this appendix, it seems to have been omitted from performances in Fletcher's lifetime. Fletcher had a reputation for overwriting, and often had to be 'pruned' by his colleagues. This scene contributes nothing to the plot but more opportunities to make fun of Moroso (a character inspired by Jonson's Morose).]

Enter PETRONIUS *and* MOROSO.

Petronius. A box o'th' ear, do you say?
Moroso.   Yes, sure, a sound one,
    Beside my nose blown to my hand. If Cupid
    Shoot arrows of that weight, I'll swear devoutly,
    He's sued his livery, and is no more a boy.
Petronius. You gave her some ill language?
Moroso.   Not a word.   5
Petronius. Or, might be, you were fumbling?
Moroso.   Would I had, sir!
    I had been aforehand then. But to be baffled

1.3.11+1 *train*] (Worn by a bride.)
+2 *say thy prayers*] (Before he goes to bed – leaving him winded even before sex might begin.)

2.0] Petronius's house.
2. *blown*] being wrung.
4. *He's . . . livery*] i.e., he is no longer an apprentice.
6. *fumbling*] groping her.
7. *aforehand*] prepared. (With a pun on a groping *hand*.)
baffled] disgraced.

177

And have no feeling of the cause –
Petronius.   Be patient.
    I have a medicine, clapped to her back, will cure her.
Moroso. No, sure, it must be afore, sir.
Petronius.   O' my conscience,   10
    When I got these two wenches (who till now
    Ne'er showed their riding) I was drunk with bastard,
    Whose nature is to form things like itself,
    Heady and monstrous. Did she slight him too?
Moroso. That's all my comfort: a mere hobbyhorse   15
    She made Childe Roland. 'Sfoot, she would not know
      him,
    Not give him a free look, nor reckon him
    Among her thoughts – which I held more than wonder,
    I having seen her within's three days kiss him
    With such an appetite as though she would eat him.   20
Petronius. There is some trick in this. How did he take it?
Moroso. Ready to cry. He ran away.
Petronius.   I fear her.
    And yet I tell you, ever to my anger
    She is as tame as innocency. It may be
    This blow was but a favour.
Moroso.   I'll be sworn   25

---

    8. *feeling*] understanding.
    9. *clapped . . . back*] applied to her back (as a poultice).
    10. *afore*] applied to her front. (Moroso mistakes Petronius as referring to anal sex or sex in the 'doggie' position, considered almost as depraved as the former.)
    11. *got*] begot.
    12. *riding*] true colours (as a horse must be tried by riding).
    bastard] sweet wine.
    14. *him*] (Roland).
    15. *hobbyhorse*] toy horse (figuratively, a fool).
    16. *Childe Roland*] (mocking Rowland by comparing him to a knight in a ballad; 'child' could refer to a wellborn youth, though here there is obviously a pun on the more general sense of the word).
    '*Sfoot*] By God's foot. (An oath.)
    17. *free*] willing.
    18. *held . . . wonder*] found exceedingly strange.
    22. *fear*] suspect.
    23. *to*] in response to.
    25. *favour*] love token.

'Twas well tied on, then.

Petronius.   Go to. Pray, forget it.
    I have bespoke a priest, and within's two hours
    I'll have ye married. Will that please you?

Moroso.   Yes.

Petronius. I'll see it done myself, and give the lady
    Such a sound exhortation for this knavery,   30
    I'll warrant you, shall make her smell this month on't.

Moroso. Nay, good sir, be not violent.

Petronius.   Neither.

Moroso.   It may be
    Out of her earnest love there grew a longing
    (As you know women have such toys) in kindness
    To give me a box o'th' ear, or so.

Petronius.   It may be.   35

Moroso. I reckon for the best still. This night, then,
    I shall enjoy her?

Petronius.   You shall handsel her.

Moroso. Old as I am, I'll give her one blow for't,
    Shall make her groan this twelvemonth.

Petronius.   Where's your jointure?

Moroso. I have a jointure for her.

Petronius.   Have your counsel perused it yet?   40

Moroso. No counsel but the night, and your sweet daughter,
    Shall e'er peruse that jointure.

Petronius.   Very well, sir.

Moroso. I'll no demurrers on't, nor no rejoinders.

---

26. *tied on*] administered. (Playing on the use of ribbons as favours tied to the hair or clothing.)
27. *bespoke*] engaged.
31. *smell*] i.e., 'scared shitless'.
32. *Neither*] I won't.
34. *toys*] tricks.
kindness] affection.
37. *handsel*] first use.
39. *groan*] (in childbirth).
jointure] marriage settlement.
40. *jointure*] sexual joining.
counsel] lawyers.
41. *counsel*] witnesses, advisors.
43. *demurrers on't*] objections to it.
rejoinders] rebuttals.

The other's ready sealed.
Petronius.   Come then, let's comfort
    My son Petruccio. He's like little children   45
    That lose their baubles, crying ripe.
Moroso.   Pray tell me,
    Is this stern woman still upon the flaunt
    Of bold defiance?
Petronius.   Still, and still she shall be,
    Till she be starved out. You shall see such justice
    That women shall be glad, after this tempest,   50
    To tie their husbands' shoes and walk their horses.
Moroso. That were a merry world! Do you hear the rumour?
    They say the women are in insurrection,
    And mean to make a [cunt-republic].
Petronius.   They'll sooner
    Draw upon walls as we do. Let 'em, let 'em.   55
    We'll ship 'em out in cuck-stools; there they'll sail
    As brave Columbus did, till they discover
    The happy islands of obedience.
    We stay too long: come.
Moroso.   Now, St George be with us!

After 2.3.77 [This passage, not present in the manuscript, may
have been intended as an apolitical alternative to 2.3.68–77. It adds
no new information, and makes the scene drag in performance.]

---

44. *other's*] other contract is.
46. *baubles*] playthings.
crying ripe] ripe for crying.
47. *stern woman*] (Maria).
54. *cunt-republic*] (1) democratic nation of women; (2) 'country-public',
nation that belongs to the people (but also punning on 'public cunt', woman
available for any man's use).
55. *Draw upon*] urinate on.
56. *cuck-stools*] chairs designed as implements of punishment and humiliation, in which the offender would be strapped and then dunked into a
pond or river. (A device frequently used on outspoken women.)
57. *Columbus*] (The discovery of the New World led to reports that a
nation consisting entirely of women – the Amazons – could be found in what
is now Brazil.)
58. *happy islands*] (Alluding to the 'Fortunate Isles' of classical and Celtic
mythology, a paradise located somewhere in the Atlantic where blest souls
went after death.)

Pedro. Then are they victualled with pies and puddings,
  (The trappings of good stomachs), noble ale
  (The true defender), sausages (and smoked ones,
  If need be, such as serve for pikes), and pork
  (Better the Jews ne'er hated), here and there   5
  A bottle of metheglin, a stout Briton
  That will stand to 'em. What else they want, they war for.

After 2.5.132 [This speech adds another joke at Moroso's expense.]

Livia. [*To Petronius*] He will undo me in mere pans of coals
  To make him lusty.

3.5.48–62 [The expansive printed version of this passage introduces two characters who take no other part in the action, and contribute nothing to the development of the scene.]

Petruccio. [*Within*]   Will ye hear me? First, be pleased
  To think I know ye all, and can distinguish
  Ev'ry man's several voice. You that spoke first   50
  I know my father-in-law; the other, Tranio;
  And I heard Sophocles; the last – pray, mark me –
  Is my damned wife Maria.
  If any man misdoubt me for infected,   53+1
          [*He thrusts his arm out.*]
  There is mine arm: let any man look on't.

      Enter Doctor *and* Apothecary.

Doctor. Save ye, gentlemen.
Petronius.   Oh welcome, doctor!
  Ye come in happy time. Pray, your opinion:
  What think you of his pulse?

 2.3.77+1. *victualled*] supplied with food.
 +3. *defender*] (because drinking it brings courage).
 +6. *metheglin*] spiced mead.
 +7. *stand to 'em*] stand by them.

 2.5.132+1–2.] Kindling his passion will bankrupt me in the cost of coalpans alone.

 3.5.53+3. *Save*] God save.
 +4. *happy*] good.
 Pray] Please give us.

Doctor. [*Feeling Petruccio's pulse*] It beats wi'th' busiest   53+5
    And shows a general inflammation,
    Which is the symptom of a pestilent fever.
    Take twenty ounces from him.
Petruccio. [*Within, withdrawing his arm*] Take a fool!
    Take an ounce from mine arm and, Doctor Deuce-ace,
    I'll make a close-stool of your velvet costard! –   53+10
    'Death, gentlemen, do ye make a May-game on me?   54
    I tell ye once again, I am as sound,
    As well, as wholesome and as sensible
    As any of ye all. Let me out quickly
    Or, as I am a man, I'll beat the walls down,
    And the first thing I light upon shall pay for't.   59
Petronius. Nay, we'll go with you, doctor.
                            Exit Doctor *and* Pothecary.
Maria.   'Tis the safest.   59+1
    I saw the tokens, sir.
Petronius.   Then there is but one way.   59+2
Petruccio. (*Within*) Will it please ye open?   62

4.0 [This scene originally began Act 4, and was followed by what
our edition – and the manuscript – identifies as 4.1. Like 2.0, it
expands the roles of the two old men; it also contains the play's only
indication that Bianca has an offstage husband (4.0.98). Without it,
Bianca represents a clearer alternative to Maria and Livia: a woman
who asserts her independence outside, rather than within,
matrimonial institutions. Much of the additional Bianca material
emphasizes that she is not responsible for Maria's behaviour, but
Fletcher's intention is clear enough in Maria's own scenes.]

Enter MOROSO *and* PETRONIUS.

Moroso. That I do love her is without all question –
    And most extremely, dearly, most exactly –

  +5. *wi'th' busiest*] very fast.
  +8. *ounces*] ounces of blood.
  Take a fool] i.e., The hell you will.
  +9. *Deuce-ace*] an unlucky throw in dice.
  +10. *close-stool*] chamber-pot.
  costard] i.e., hat.

  4.0] Petronius's house.

And that I would even now, this present Monday,
Before all others, maids, wives, women, widows,
Of what degree or calling, marry her,   5
As certain too. But to be made a whimwham,
A jibcrack, and a gentleman o' the first house,
For all my kindness to her –
Petronius.   How you take it!
    Thou get a wench, thou get a dozen night-caps.
    Wouldst have her come and lick thee like a calf   10
    And blow thy nose and buss thee?
Moroso.   Not so, neither.
Petronius. What wouldst thou have her do?
Moroso.   Do as she should do:
    Put on a clean smock, and to church and marry,
    And then to bed, o' God's name! This is fair play,
    And keeps the king's peace. Let her leave her bobs   15
    (I have had too many of them) and her quillets.
    She is as nimble that way as an eel;
    But in the way she ought, to me especially,
    A sow of lead is swifter.
Petronius.   Quote your griefs down.
Moroso. Give fair quarter. I am old and crazy   20
    And subject to much fumbling, I confess it;
    Yet something I would have that's warm, to hatch me.
    But understand me, I would have it so

---

6. *As*] is as
whimwham] plaything.
7. *jibcrack*] butt of jokes.
first house] highest rank (probably sarcastic, as in Shakespeare's *Romeo and Juliet* 2.4.24).
9. *night-caps*] (i.e., cuckold's horns.)
11. *buss*] kiss.
15. *the king's peace*] i.e., law and order.
bobs] tricks.
16. *quillets*] quibbles.
18. *way she ought*] duty she owes.
19. *sow*] (1) ingot (2) female pig.
Quote] Make note of.
20. *Give fair quarter*] Make allowances.
crazy] addled.
22. *hatch*] i.e., make young again.
23. *so*] so that.

I buy not more repentance in the bargain
Than the ware's worth I have. If you allow me   25
Worthy your son-in-law and your allowance,
Do it a way of credit; let me show so,
And not be troubled in my visitations
With blows and bitterness and downright railings,
As if we were to couple the two cats   30
With clawing and loud clamour.

Petronius.   Thou fond man,
Hast thou forgot the ballad 'Crabbèd age'?
Can May and January match together,
And never a storm between 'em? Say she abuse thee;
Put case she do.

Moroso.   Well?

Petronius.   Nay, believe she does.   35

Moroso. I do believe she does.

Petronius.   And devilishly.
Art thou a whit the worse?

Moroso.   That's not the matter.
I know, being old, 'tis fit I am abused;
I know 'tis handsome, and I know moreover
I am to love her for't.

Petronius.   Now you come to me.   40

Moroso. Nay, more than this: I find too, and find certain,
What gold I have, pearl, bracelets, rings, or ouches,
Or what she can desire, gowns, petticoats,
Waistcoats, embroidered stockings, scarves, cawls,
    feathers,

---

25. *I have*] that I have.
31. *fond*] foolish.
32. *'Crabbèd Age'*] a ballad that begins 'Crabbèd age and youth cannot live together. Youth is full of pleasure, age is full of care.'
34. *Say*] Suppose.
abuse] scolds.
35. *Put case*] Suppose.
believe] imagine.
37. *a whit*] at all.
38. *fit*] fitting that.
39. *'tis*] she is.
40. *come to me*] i.e., talk sense.
42. *ouches*] brooches.
44. *cawls*] hair-nets.

  Hats, five-pound garters, muffs, masks, ruffs and ribbons, 45
  I am to give her for't.
Petronius.   'Tis right, you are so.
Moroso. But when I have done all this, and think it duty,
  Is't requisite another bore my nostrils?
  Riddle me that.
Petronius.   Go, get you gone, and dream
  She's thine within these two days, for she is so. 50
  The boy's beside the saddle. Get warm broths
  And feed apace. Think not of worldly business;
  It cools the blood. Leave off your tricks, they are hateful,
  And mere forerunners of the ancient measures.
  Contrive your beard o' the top cut, like *verdugo*s; 55
  It shows you would be wise. And burn your night-cap;
  It looks like half a winding sheet, and urges
  From a young wench nothing but cold repentance.
  You may eat onions, so you'll not be lavish.
Moroso. I am glad of that.
Petronius.   They purge the blood and quicken. 60
  But, after 'em – conceive me – sweep your mouth
  And, where there wants a tooth, stick in a clove.
Moroso. Shall I hope once again? Say't.
Petronius.   You shall, sir –
  And you shall have your hope.
Moroso.   Why, there's a match, then.

    Enter BIANCA *and* TRANIO.

---

 45. *five-pound*] i.e., costly.
 48. *bore my nostrils*] i.e., cuckold me.
 51. *The . . . saddle*] i.e., All is ready.
 52. *apace*] promptly and well.
 53. *tricks*] mannerisms.
 54. *ancient measures*] old-fashioned dances.
 55.] Contrive to cut your beard in a long and narrow shape (a Spanish fashion).
 57. *winding sheet*] shroud.
 59. *so*] provided.
lavish] excessive.
 60. *quicken*] enliven.
 61. *conceive*] understand.
sweep] cleanse.
 62. *wants*] lacks.

Bianca. [*Aside to Tranio*] You shall not find me wanting. Get
    you gone.   65
    Here's the old man. He'll think you are plotting else
    Something against his new son.   *Exit* TRANIO.
Moroso. [*To Petronius*]   Fare you well, sir.   *Exit.*
Bianca. [*Sings*] An every buck had his doe
    And every cuckold a bell at his toe,
    Oh, what sport should we have then, then, boys, then,   70
    Oh, what sport should we have then!
Petronius. [*Aside*] This is the spirit that inspires 'em all.
Bianca. Give you good even.
Petronius.   A word with you, sweet lady.
Bianca. I am very hasty, sir.
Petronius.   So you were ever.
Bianca. Well, what's your will?
Petronius.   Was not your skilful hand   75
    In this last stratagem? Were not your mischiefs
    Eking the matter on?
Bianca.   In's shutting up?
    Is that it?
Petronius.   Yes.
Bianca.   I'll tell you.
Petronius.   Do.
Bianca.   And truly.
    Good old man, I do grieve exceeding much,
    I fear too much –
Petronius.   I am sorry for your heaviness.   80
    Belike you can repent, then?
Bianca.   There you are wide too. –
    Not that the thing was done (conceive me rightly)

---

  68. *An*] If.
  72. *'em all*] (the women).
  74. *very hasty*] in great haste.
  So . . . ever] You were always that way.
  77. *Eking*] urging.
  In's] In his (Petruccio's).
  80. *heaviness*] grief.
  81. *Belike*] Perhaps.
  wide] wide of the mark.

Does any way molest me.
Petronius.   What, then, lady?
Bianca. But that I was not in it, there's my sorrow.
  There, now you understand me. For, I'll tell you,   85
  It was so sound a piece, and so well carried,
  And – if you mark the way – so handsomely,
  Of such a height and excellence and art
  I have not known a braver; for (conceive me)
  When the gross fool her husband would be sick –   90
Petronius. Pray, stay –
Bianca.   (Nay, good, your patience) – and no sense for't,
  Then stepped your daughter in –
Petronius.   By your appointment.
Bianca. (I would it had, on that condition
  I had but one half-smock, I like it so well!)
  – And, like an excellent cunning woman, cured me   95
  One madness with another, which was rare
  And, to our weak beliefs, a wonder.
Petronius.   Hang you!
  For surely, if your husband look not to you,
  I know what will.
Bianca.   I humbly thank Your Worship,
  And so I take my leave.
Petronius.   You have a hand, I hear too –   100
Bianca. I have two, sir.
Petronius. In my young daughter's business.
Bianca. You will find there

---

83. *molest*] bother.
86. *piece*] plot.
carried] carried off.
89. *braver*] finer.
91. *sense*] explanation.
92. *appointment*] direction.
93–4. *I . . . half-smock*] i.e., I would give almost anything to have had a hand in it.
95. *cunning woman*] female healer. (Distinguished from university-trained male doctors.)
99. *I . . . will*] i.e., She will pay one way or another for her behaviour. (The ambiguity of the threat might be clarified in performance.)

       A fitter hand than mine to reach her frets
       And play down-diddle to her.
Petronius.   I shall watch you.   105
Bianca. Do.
Petronius. And I shall have justice.
Bianca.   Where?
Petronius.   That's all one.
       I shall be with you at a turn henceforward.
Bianca. Get you a posset too. And so good even, sir.

                                   Exeunt [*severally*].

After 5.1.36 [The information about her repenting is repeated
shortly after.]

Petronius.   Yes, sir –
       Or rather, as it seems, repenting. And there
       She lies within, debating on't.
Roland.   Well, sir?

   104–5. *A . . . her*] (1) another hand than mine can play her (sexual)
instrument better (frets are the sections on the fingerboard of a stringed
instrument, the fiddle represents the female genitals, and 'down-diddle' is a
ballad refrain with bawdy implications); (2) another (probably Roland) can
better manage her fretful behaviour.
   105. *watch*] keep an eye on.
   106. *That's all one*] i.e. Never you mind.
   107. *with . . . turn*] even with you.
   108. *posset*] hot medicinal cordial.

   5.1.36+2. *debating*] reflecting.